PRAISE FOR *GENERATION CREATION*:

"It's so pretty."
MISSY REITNER-CAMERON

"ABSOLUTELY THE BEST BOOK I NEVER READ!"
KEN ALTERWITZ

"I visit AdVerve for the hardcore porn, mostly."
DAVID GIANATASIO

"WAITING FOR THE MOVIE."
TODD SANDERS

"This book taught me SO MUCH about knitting, that I was able to... wait, wrong book review. I didn't read this one, sorry."
CHRIS BRYANT

"PART OF A BALANCED LUNCH."
JEFF KWIATEK

"There are a lot of words in this book. And a few of them are pretty good!"
DIANNE HANLON DRUYFF

"DEFINITELY NOT ENOUGH UGC IN THIS EDITION."
ERIC FLEMING

"Buy it otherwise it won't be sold."
FRÉDÉRIC-GÉRARD LEVEQUE

"I'D LIKE TO ADD YOU TO MY PROFESSIONAL NETWORK ON LINKEDIN."
DAN WEINGROD

"If you judge by the quotes on the cover, this is a great book."
CHRISTOPHE LAUER

"SIGNIFICANTLY BETTER THAN A STICK IN THE EYE."
CAITLIN SCHILLER

"First."
MICHAEL BOAMAH

"IT'S GOTTA BE WAY BETTER THAN TRUMP'S BOOK."
JACKY SAULNIER

"They paid me absolutely no money to say something about this book."
JANE GOLDMAN

"SOME GUY ON THE INTERNET SAID IT'S THE BEST BOOK HE'S EVER READ. — (SIGNED) SOME GUY ON THE INTERNET."
ADAM KUHR

"Ever read a transcript of a podcast? Me neither. But that's what you'll find inside."
DAN GOLDGEIER

"THEIR FIRST EDITION 'HOW TO SUCCESS- FULLY LAND THE PERFECT JOB WHILE SPEAKING A DEAD LANGUAGE' GOT RAVE REVIEWS FROM SOMEONE OR ANOTHER."
MAUREEN-ALEX HORTON

"I check your blog more than I work."
KYM DAVIS

"JUST LIKE TINDER, YOU CAN KEEP SWIPING RIGHT WITH THIS READ."
CAT TURNER

"I read this at work and got promoted. Then fired."
ANDREW LOOS

"SOCIAL NETWORKS ARE SUCH GREAT PLACES FOR BRAINSUCKING."
WAI-MING LUNG

"This book may include whimsical scenarios with colorful dragons. You decide because I've had enough peyote this week."
WENDY PINKO CAHILL

"THE TARGET AUDIENCE FOR THIS BOOK IS MALES AND FEMALES, AGED ZERO AND UP."
GEORGE TURNER

Bill Green   Angela Natividad   Darryl Ohrt

TO OUR YOUNGER SELVES.

Intro V

CREATIVITY IN LIFE

1. What does creativity mean? 4

2. Is storytelling dead? 8

3. How do you be creative when everything's
    already been done? 14

4. What's your creative process? 18

5. Are there things that you have to do before you
    can start being creative? 26

6. How do you stay creative? 32

7. How do you bring creativity into personal pursuits? 38

8. Does your main creative focus inform the
    rest of your life? 44

9. How do you manage money? 48

10. What do you do when your head gets in the way? 52

11. Do you give a fuck? 56

12. What about boredom? 62

13. What's your take on Mad Men? 66

14. Who's more important—the creator or the curator? 72

15. Can you create in the suburbs? 78

16. Is it possible to grow analog creative in a
    digital world? 84

17. Who's your creative idol? 90

18. Do you have a muse? 96

19. What are your demons? 100

20. What clothes or totems make you feel creative? 104

21. Are there any places that make you feel especially creative? 110

22. What is all this for? 114

CREATIVITY IN BUSINESS

23. Do you feel like working in advertising is selling out? 120

24. How do you keep current? 124

25. What ingredients do you need to start a successful agency? 128

26. What's more important—chemistry or culture? 132

27. How do you create culture? 136

28. What makes a creative environment? 144

29. How big is the perfect agency? 148

30. Does collaboration work when it comes to creativity? 152

31. How many people are the right creative mix? 158

32. Who shouldn't be on a creative team? 164

33. What do you do when there's just no spark? 170

34. Is the 10,000 hours thing true? 174

35. How many hours are too many hours? 180

36. Is it important to believe in the idea? 188

37. Who are you accountable to? 192

38. What's the creative director's job? 196

39. What's the role of an account person on a
     creative team? 200

40. What are briefs good for anyway? 206

41. How do you produce for audiences? 212

42. What do you do when there's not enough
     money to sustain the idea? 216

43. What is wrong with the agency/client
     relationship? 220

44. Have you ever taken one for the team? 226

45. When were you financially taken advantage of? 232

46. Have you ever been ripped off creatively? 236

47. Can a successful creative culture be imported
     to a satellite agency? 244

48. Where do you find the will to do stuff that
     doesn't interest you? 248

49. Do you procrastinate? 252

50. How long to procrastinate? 256

51. How do you manage creative adversity? 260

52. How do you cultivate creativity in a negative environment?.. 266

53. How do you deal with failure?................................. 270

54. How do you know when you've gotten too comfortable?................. 274

55. Have you got a Plan B?... 278

56. When do you walk away? 282

57. When do you pursue new things? 290

58. Would you do it all again? 298

CREATIVE HORIZONS

Last words before bowing out 308

Acknowledgments 314

Why should
I listen to advice
from you?

Why should you listen to advice from anyone, really? One of the cool things you'll see in this book is that there are no definitive answers, no one way to creative success. The beauty of seeing perspectives from three souls spread across three countries, performing three different roles in the creative industry, is that everyone is finding their way through this life differently. I believe in listening to (and learning from) people who have experienced life.

As for me, I created a dream career entirely by accident. I started in the music business, running an in-house agency. More than a decade later, I left to launch my own agency. Without a single client. What started as Plaid was re-branded as Humongo and eventually sold to an MDC Partners agency, then became part of a bigger ad network. At some point in the process, I got married. Had kids. Got divorced. I eventually found my soulmate, the woman I've looked for all my life, and got married. I moved to NYC to become Executive Creative Director at Carrot Creative.

During my tenure there, they more than doubled in size and won their biggest pitches in history. I eventually left Carrot to found Mash+Studio, one of New York City's first social content studios. I left NYC to move to Berlin and eventually Bavaria. I've worked with agencies all over the world, big and small. Over my career, I've had the fortune of working on fantastic brands that include Timex, Segway, BIC, Target, Home Depot, Jaguar, Marc Jacobs and Hermès.

People in our industry are defined by the titles they've held and the brand names they've worked on, so maybe that'll impress you. I'm more proud of the work done and the relationships formed. But that's just me.

Everything that follows is based on some hard-fought years working for all types of agencies—good and bad. It's the advice I've given both my daughter, who is also in the industry, and my son, who is not. Which means it can be brutal at times and practical at others, but always honest, because, well, I love you all like my children. Most of you.

I started out life as a designer fresh out of UConn, working my way up through a generation of post-Mad Men agency types at several boutique shops in the NYC area. More interested in chasing popular brands than agencies, my path to this point ended up taking a lot of left turns. Along the way, I got some awards and a few war stories, and helped more than a few shops make a lot of money, be it through new business wins or keeping an unhappy client from walking out the door.

Name a Fortune 500 brand and I've likely worked on it. In a business that needs its silos and labels, I call myself art director, writer, strategist, new business development person, social media whatever, and—last but not least—friend to Darryl and Angela. The cynic in me could say I'll be whatever you need me to be if the money's right. The hopeful kid right out of school would say I still love this industry and coming up with ideas, because that's what it's all about.

I've had the opportunity to work with Darryl while he was at Plaid, and have also worked on pitches with Angela. Smart people, them. Both Darryl and I follow similar trajectories as far as relationships go. Why does that matter? Because I've also discovered along the way the degree to which relationships matter most both in your personal and professional side; it's not just about budgets or making your logo bigger.

It's this filter that informs what follows in the chapters ahead, because no matter how this business has changed and how fast technology evolves, the three of us still see brands and agencies make the same mistakes over and over. And they're not doing anything about it.

 Before a small, soon-to-be-national startup made me its marketing director and got the wheels turning on my career, I was their CSR girl, so glad to be out of Sunglass Hut that I didn't want to go home on the weekends; I wanted to be there, doing data entry. Impressed by my obvious desire to become a robot, they put me in front of their PPC campaigns and the rest was history; I was found.

If you recognize my name, maybe it's because you read Adrants. My biggest fear then was getting called out for not actually working in the industry. So I made a point of doing that, and finally understood why it's so hard to produce good work. Today I'm a strategist, international account director, copywriter, ad blogger, and editor, who's been living in Paris for the last seven years. (Another crazy story in and of itself.) My LinkedIn looks like I either can't make up my mind, or have trouble saying no (both of those things are true). At night, I write this book with two of my best friends in the world.

But this isn't really about what we've done. It's about how we think, and whether we were able to walk that delicate line between having lots of work, or being mindful of the work we do and using it to carve out the life we wanted to live in. (I suppose that's what determines creative success.) Sometimes we did this well; a lot of times it was harder, and more than once, we made it more complicated than it needed to be.

But writing this book, then rereading it, reminded me that creativity isn't a crayon that some kids get and others don't; it's so innate, so spontaneously natural, that we often don't see it. It'll provide just enough inspiration to guide you to a solution that seems evident once found. It colors the menagerie of missions we fill our days with, elevating pithy jokes, painstakingly crafted throwaway blogs, and lazy margin doodles into a moment's worth of art. It's the little nagging itch that sometimes tells us what we're doing won't cut it anymore; you need something new. That its fruits don't always last doesn't mean it was never there, or that it didn't matter. It's proof of life—a sublime spark of sentience in the machine.

I'm not sure I'm in the position to give advice. But I can tell you you're creative, whether you feel that way or not. So maybe you'll see yourself somewhere in here, and it'll feel like you found your people. Maybe that'll be enough to strike out and make what you want, regardless of what you fear it might cost. (Often it won't cost as much as you stand to gain.)

OVER THE LAST YEAR, ANGELA WAS SECRETLY SCREEN CAPTURING
EACH OF OUR WEEKLY SKYPE CALLS.

1

creativit

y in life

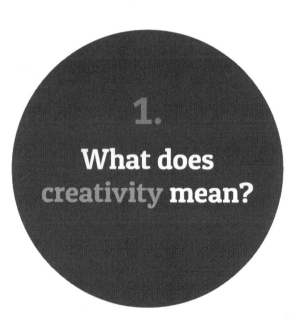

1.

What does creativity mean?

To create

you have to

wonder what's

possible.

This is like looking directly into the sun. I think cultivating a desire to know, explore and discover, letting yourself go down pointless paths and get lost sometimes, makes you creative. To be creative, to create, you have to wonder what's possible.

 I believe that creative people have a manner at looking at the world and seeing things differently. You can walk down a path with a "normal" person, and they'll see the path, and the trees along the way. Maybe they'll see the grass and the cyclist. The "creative" person sees the way the sunlight is diffused by the trees, the shadows it creates in the grass and the way it accentuates the glisten of the cyclist's bike. They see the whole thing as a painted scene and think, "That would be perfect for _____."

 This is a question that seems to get harder and harder to answer. I like to think in its simplest form, creativity is how we respond to a particular stimulus or challenge. (And by "we," I mean everyone.) I'm as democratic about this as Darryl is: Everyone sees the world differently and responds to creativity in their own way, be it engineer, artist or accountant.

Epic soul-searching—with large amounts of caffeine— have formed at least one core belief about creativity that

I can't shake: It's hard for me to say one person's way of seeing is any less valid than another's. All creatives deal with competition in one form or another, yet I firmly believe that everyone has a right to express the way they see the world in their own creative way.

Every day, people in seemingly inartistic fields deal creatively with what they're confronted with. Is the team of NASA engineers, who figured out how to get the Apollo 13 crew back to Earth, any less creative than coders dying to debug a website feature?

Creativity can exist for its own sake, or become a means to a problem-solving end. Is creative inherently a result of form, function, or both? To deny someone the right to express how they see the world denies their very being, even if we disagree with the quality of the execution or the medium they express themselves in.

"MAKING THE SIMPLE COMPLICATED IS COMMONPLACE; MAKING THE COMPLICATED SIMPLE, AWESOMELY SIMPLE, THAT'S CREATIVITY."
CHARLES MINGUS

2.

Is storytelling dead?

Not everybody is a storyteller.

Not everybody is a storyteller; it's as much art as science. I hate hearing from thought leaders who say "Content is King." No, **great** content is king. **Any** content simply doesn't cut it.

 Humans need stories like food. Did you ever hear that pop-science thing about how we're hard-wired to see little faces in electrical outlets? We're always hunting for omens, signs, proof there's a running narrative that will guide us down the right path if we can just find it. It's how we make connections, part of what we are.

We'll always need stories to make sense of who we are. Zia Haider Raiman even said, once, that stories are dangerous: "The day someone thought of calling pigeons flying rats was the day the fate of pigeons was sealed."

 Every generation loves to declare things dead. Storytelling will never die, but that doesn't mean it's not susceptible to illness. Storytelling across social media is suffering—from a sea of *me-too publishers* hosing us with content, a narcissistic population that can't see enough photos of themselves, and from mediocrity.

It's not that there isn't fantastic storytelling happening; it's just so deeply buried in a mountain of the "any content" Bill mentioned that we can't find it. It's getting harder to source great content. For a while, this was an opportunity—but the so-called "curators" have since been purchased by conglomerates driven by clicks, killing off the quality of what rises to the top.

I dream that the selfie generation will tire of seeking Likes, the content curators will die of clickbait poisoning, and the truly gifted creators will rise to the top.

But it's cyclical though, right? We're living in an age where almost all kids pirate and don't even know it's wrong. Every place you look is throwing content at you; even Snapchat is trying to make web series. (If those take off and Snapchat becomes a kind of seconds-long Netflix... wow, this is going to sound really dated.) Surprisingly (or not), demand for better production is rising across the board. The more people are hosed, the more they have to consume, the more selective they become. Complexity and finesse are valorised again.

There is so much bad stuff out there. But it's also such a great time to be a storyteller, to sell rich and inventive ideas, because there are so many takers now, and they've won the luxury of being pickier. We have to take advantage of this time to explore those more gratifying storylines and less obvious connections—and we can in ways we couldn't when just a few people were deciding what we watched and consumed.

We often forget that shit is fertile soil for elaborate orchids, or even just really nice potatoes. Did I ruin this metaphor?

 Metaphor intact, and taken further: Fertile soil is meaningless without love and water. Speaking of dated, and to demonstrate the internet's circle of life and why books about it will never keep up, Snapchat has disbanded its original content division since Angela mentioned it.

 Le sigh. Guess I should've seen that coming.

"STORYTELLING IS MY CURRENCY."

KEVIN SMITH

3.

How can you be creative when everything's already been done?

Ideas

are

endless.

You can't be creative if you remember every idea's already been hashed out and iterated. What you can do is remember that no one else's treatment of it will be quite like yours. In much wiser words from Ghost in the Shell 2: Innocence, "What the body creates is as much an expression of its DNA as the body itself."

The trick isn't necessarily to invent something that never existed; that severely limits your options. Focus on differentiating your approach. In the how and in the doing, you'll reveal who you are—and maybe that'll resonate with others.

There's data to back this up: the most creative and innovative industries are those unhindered by copyright, meaning people can copy without shame and build on one another's ideas constantly: Fashion, gaming, and automotive are just a few. You don't have to be an unbridled originator; just keep building **better**.

Stop stressing over everything. Yeah, yeah, everything's been done before. No idea is original. If you discover your brilliant idea has been done by someone else, move on to idea #2. Or twist it to the point where it's no longer recognizable as idea #1. Ideas are endless. Stop crying over what other people have done, and just keep moving.

Everything we see is a result of many influences coming together—be it a startup growth-hacked off a different app, or an indie band that gets famous covering an old song from a singer you never heard of. I never worry about running out of ideas, mostly because we are wildly variable creatures with a seemingly unending supply of mashable fodder to work from.

Formats and genres may be similar, but it's what we do with those parameters that make this trip worth the price. Miles had the same 12 notes to work with as Miley, but you tell me who did more with them. Before you answer, let's get extra fancy and throw sales into the mix: Is an artist more or less of an artist because they're popular and sell a ton of mediocre work?

"THAT IS WHAT THE MODERN SEARCH IS FOR: WHERE TO GO NEXT."   THEODORE ZELDIN

4.

What's your creative process?

"Everyone vote for

your favorite idea"

is a sure way

to mediocrity.

I read *What I Talk About When I Talk About Running* about a year ago, then took up running because I became convinced that that's what I needed to do to write a book (as opposed to, say, writing one). I didn't get the outcome hoped for, but I now feel it is vital to keep running. My head clears, I can be alone with my thoughts, and it's probably the only time I don't feel a nagging urgency to meet Deadline X.

There's something about physical activity that provides the headspace and energy to take all this stuff you've absorbed, let it float about on its own without you poking it, then go make something out of it. After running, my head is full of notes and things I'm ready to do. For me, it's become the best and most reliable way to drag the fickle Muse, kicking and screaming, back to me.

Also, make time for sleep. Seriously. Let your brain do its work while your cells take time to repair; it's the best way to wake up ready to grab a pen.

Wow, Angela just perfectly summed up what it means to be a runner. I have the exact experience at the end of almost every run. I also like that while I'm running, I'm rarely attempting to solve a particular problem, but feel free to explore whatever happens in my head. And it's hard to find time for that kind of headspace in our day-to-day lives. We've created a world where it's no longer acceptable to just sit down and think. Running provides that opportunity.

I do have a process for the workplace, however, and believe it's important for every creative director to work this out. The best process is going to be different for every creative leader. I've found that I prefer two brainstorms for every challenge, with strict rules: They can't last longer than 60 minutes, participants cannot denounce an idea for any reason, there should never be more than five people in the room, and I could care less if participants read the brief.

Sometimes brilliance is found in the first brainstorm. Making time for a second one in every production schedule allows for further exploration, and this is important regardless of what genius is invented in the first meeting. A second brainstorm lets you get past the first 50 ideas that everyone thinks of. It allows you to explore paths you might have missed in the first. It will save the day when you come up empty after a day when people just weren't hitting it.

After successful brainstorming, I believe it's the creative director's role to hone down the winning ideas worthy of being fleshed out into full-blown concepts. This cannot be done with group consensus. "Everyone vote for your favorite idea" is a sure way to mediocrity. Copywriters and strategists are perfect partners for fleshing out ideas and making them real. More importantly–they can help bring what seems like an outlandish concept into the realm of matching the brief, and solving the problem. And that's what it's about at the end of the day, right?

 Procrastination is my process. I serve at its pleasure, sans guilt. No matter what the deadline–two hours, two weeks or two months–I can't jump in and focus on the thing (whatever the thing is) without first doing things wholly unrelated to it. If my desk is messy when I want to sit and write a proposal, I'm cleaning that up first. What? The client needs it by 5:00 pm? No worries–but first, I'm watching this YouTube clip.

There are a few things at work that I use to justify this process. First, I suspect most creatives don't gravitate towards getting it done sooner rather than later. It provides no spark, none of the drama or tension that we seem to need in our lives. Secondly, we tend to think that doing the task at hand will more be difficult than it actually is. Graphic artist Gosho Aoyama once said, "Fear of death is worse than death itself." That's a darker, albeit fancier, way of saying the same thing. But the unknowns of something tend to paralyze our will to overcome them. You've probably felt this way when approaching a subject you don't know much about and can't seem to find a way into.

Lastly, and perhaps most importantly, I know how long something takes from years of honing and refining my work process. It's why I'm confident in my ability to sit down and bang it out, especially if it's something I've dealt with before.

 It's overwhelming to look at a huge brief or a series of tasks as one big block, so I break it down into manageable buckets: Easy vs Hard.

Often the list of hards isn't that long, so Easy gets broken down again into Quick to Accomplish versus Slow as Fuck. Slow as Fucks I delegate if possible—creatives for example can already start ideating while a strategist and planner work on demographics, tonality and other skeletal aspects. Once fast-moving Easies are knocked out, 40-60% of the work is handled.

To save time, it helps to have a set of slides that outline already your story: Intro to the Agency (rarely needs changing), Problem, Research, Insight, Solution, KPIs, Awesome Finish. Even if the order of stuff changes later, you basically always need these seven things.

Writing articles is even simpler: I do a freewrite where I say everything I want to on the subject, then elaborate on each point. That gives you all the "puzzle pieces." Once you have the puzzle pieces, it's easier to see the shape things should take. You can move the puzzle pieces around and kill all your darlings.

"THE PROCESS WITH MANY ARTISTS IS QUICK...
NOT, HOWEVER, WITH ME."

PETER GABRIEL

"THE CREATIVE PROCESS IS A PROCESS OF SURRENDER, NOT CONTROL."   JULIA CAMERON

"ALL THE BEST IDEAS COME OUT OF THE PROCESS; THEY COME OUT OF THE WORK ITSELF."

CHUCK CLOSE

5.

Are there things you have to do before you can start being creative?

It all starts

with a

blank page.

Running twice a week. I need a pen and notebook nearby at all times, including by my bed. I keep separate notebooks for personal and professional stuff, and the professional one has a table of contents I can fill out so I can jump to old notes fast. Also, I use a Sheaffer fountain pen, which I've had for a few years, because I know how it feels and how it will behave. It's high-quality and relatively inexpensive for what it is. I fucking hate shitty pens, or using someone else's, even for something as basic as signing for packages.

Before I start work, I make tea, light a candle, turn on some wordless Spotify music (which somehow always tends to lead me to something from the Lord of the Rings soundtrack) and review the briefs without thinking about what was discussed the day before. Then I go over the notes from the previous day and add my fresh thoughts to them.

There's just something about the act of touching paper that makes me feel like, okay, I can do this. And this ritual is important to me because the preparation of it ensures I'm not coming back into the work with some baggage or neurotic thoughts from whatever I was doing right before it. Finding ways to compartmentalize physically makes it easier for your brain to follow suit.

A blank page. Preferably in Google Docs. It doesn't matter where I'm at, what the challenge is, how horrific the deadline. It all starts with a blank page. Once I can muster the courage to put something down on that page, it all flows from there. I don't believe that I've ever stared down a blank page for more than a few seconds. I don't mean that as a brag, because the first things on my page are always crap, but the threat of the blank page is all I need to begin digging in.

 If something works, I stick with it, so I'll use the same answer as the one I gave for defining my creative process: Procrastination.

Barring that, I have two very specific and personal deal-breakers when it comes to getting the right vibe. The first is the physical space around me. I need it free of clutter or I will feel restricted and not be relaxed enough to focus.

The second is sound. If I'm writing, I need it to be fairly quiet in the immediate area. That's hard to do in a busy studio, of course, and it's why writers tend to seek out private offices with doors—to shut out that one person who always plays their music too loud or is having a conference call with their door open for the entire office to hear.

Headphones isolate the world and allow me to focus. Any music with lyrics competes with my inner voice, so instrumental stuff it is. If the work is straight-up "get-'er-done" stuff that doesn't require intense concentration, then anything with a driving beat is fine. It's also not unusual for me to have the same song on repeat for an entire day. I shall not reveal the names of said tracks, for they are in GPWL (Guilty Pleasure Witness Relocation).

"— YOU KNOW, I'VE EITHER HAD A FAMILY, A JOB, SOMETHING
HAS ALWAYS BEEN IN THE
WAY
BUT NOW
I'VE SOLD MY HOUSE, I'VE FOUND THIS
PLACE, A LARGE STUDIO, YOU SHOULD SEE THE **SPACE** AND
THE **LIGHT**.
FOR THE FIRST TIME IN MY LIFE I'M GOING TO HAVE A PLACE AND
THE TIME TO
CREATE."

NO BABY, IF YOU'RE GOING TO CREATE
YOU'RE GOING TO CREATE WHETHER YOU WORK
16 HOURS A DAY IN A COAL MINE
OR
YOU'RE GOING TO CREATE IN A SMALL ROOM WITH 3 CHILDREN
WHILE YOU'RE ON
WELFARE,
YOU'RE GOING TO CREATE WITH PART OF YOUR MIND AND YOUR
BODY BLOWN
AWAY,
YOU'RE GOING TO CREATE BLIND
CRIPPLED
DEMENTED,
YOU'RE GOING TO CREATE WITH A CAT CRAWLING UP YOUR
BACK WHILE
THE WHOLE CITY TREMBLES IN EARTHQUAKE, BOMBARDMENT,
FLOOD AND FIRE.
BABY, AIR AND LIGHT AND TIME AND SPACE
HAVE NOTHING TO DO WITH IT
AND DON'T CREATE ANYTHING
EXCEPT MAYBE A LONGER LIFE TO FIND
NEW EXCUSES
FOR.

CHARLES BUKOWSKI • AIR AND LIGHT AND TIME AND SPACE

6.

How do you
stay creative?

Be curious.

It's not just passion that informs your work; your quirky interests do, too. Random knowledge might even inform your greatest work.

Advertising is rigorous, and its ephemeral nature means it's one of the hardest storytelling crafts: You need full, clear concepts that can be understood in an instant, and even if they're a hit, you're back to square one the next day for somebody else (or maybe the same client, who got bored). So you need to have a lot of references.

Get all the help you can. Let things happen to you. Let yourself happen to stuff. And dig! I indulge my curiosity in anything that gives me a brain itch, from the origin of "potato bug" to how to conduct a rhinoplasty step-by-step (it's actually kind of easy). And when hanging out with people I don't know that well or am working with for the first time, I like asking questions they won't expect (an old standby: "Do you think you would be a competent assassin?"); I want to hear the off-script answers that will tell me who they really are, and how they think. I document interesting findings in writing. It's shocking what you end up drawing from.

But beware of overstimulation; I read someplace that we're now ingesting as much data in a day as a previous generation did in a year. Get your insights out someplace safe, be it Evernote or in a whole collection of matchy Moleskines. Then give yourself permission to forget, to breathe. Rest your eyes and head, and let space exist between all your data hunts. To make the right connections, your mind also needs time to wander.

 I can't stay creative if I'm not curious or if I'm bored. Like speed, you can't coach curious. You either are or you're not. And if you aren't naturally curious about life, how can you be interested in anything? Asking "Why?" or "How?" takes you places that invariably end up being far more interesting than if you hadn't.

I love finding the hidden things in the negative space where people aren't looking. That only happens because I'm curious. For any interview I've done, I have a set of go-to questions ready to ask. But it's always been the insight or small detail in their answers that I can't wait to jump on, so I can make a left-hand turn that really makes it interesting. It takes the discussion in a new direction, and makes it better than I could ever have planned.

Experience shapes my curiosity. You can and should learn from all your experiences in life, good or bad, and you can always learn something you can use next time.

I agree with Bill: Experience. Experience at every level.

Experience with people: Add people to your circle. Hang out with people you don't normally spend time with. Be with people that are older, younger, richer, poorer, hipper, unemployed, recovering, on top of their game, and everything in between. You'll be surprised what new perspectives you'll gain.

The 'Jesus' strategy. I dig it.

Experience with place: We fall into routines too easily. Jumping out of these, even only for a moment, brings new perspectives, understanding and ideas. Take a different route to work. Sleep outside. Work from a lobby or coffee shop. Explore a store for something you have no interest in. Expanding your world is important; it's too easy to keep going about things the same exact way.

Experience with things: Touch things. Play with things. Learn how things work. Explore media you typically don't watch or listen to. Ride a bike instead of driving a car. Read three magazines you've never heard of before. Shop for stuff that disgusts you. Expand your boundaries.

Experience with life: We've all heard the "say yes more

often" mantra. It works. When you're bogged down in life, it feels like there are a gazillion obstacles that get in the way of exploring new things. Find time. Make time. Do things you never thought you'd do, didn't think you had time to do, or were too scared, embarrassed, or too old, too young, or too inexperienced to do.

"WHAT I NEED IN ORDER TO STAY CREATIVE AND CENTERED IS A CERTAIN AMOUNT OF DISTANCE FROM THE MADDING CROWD. YOU CEASE TO BE YOUR BEST SELF IF YOU'RE RUNNING TOO FAST."

JAMES REDFIELD

7.

How do you bring creativity into personal pursuits?

We notice

everything.

We bring the totality of what we are to the table, whatever we're doing. And in the same ways external stimuli and learnings inform our work, our work informs things we do for fun. Maybe that's how a passing interest becomes a passion, or a secret metier. (To wit: My love of TV, books and movies totally prepared me for working at an entertainment agency like Darewin, and now I'm helping build an esports agency, nurtured by my co-founder's love of CounterStrike and my boyfriend's obsession with Hearthstone.)

In fact, it's interesting to see whether you can let yourself be creative outside work without turning it into work. Case in point: For vacation this summer I bought a passel of adult coloring books. I had this fantasy of myself coloring over tables and picnic blankets like a happy kid, being 'restfully' creative and whimsical. But when I opened that book to the first tropical bird, I totally panicked: What colors to use, where to start, what if I make a mistake? In the back of the book, a highlighted artist had done the stupid bird up with oils, giving it nice lifelike effects, which was paralyzing: I no longer felt like the colored pencils I chose were the right kinds of tools.

By the time I'd learned to let go and just bloody color, I was already home. I'd made it a goddamn job.

It's a blessing and a curse. The world viewed through a creative person's eyes is a wondrous, magical place, ripe with opportunity. It's also a world that's fraught with bad typography, poor presentation and really, really horrific marketing. We notice everything.

Let's say that we're going out to dinner. A creative person enters the restaurant, and observes the style of the decor and lighting, critiquing the menu copy and forming a hypothesis on what attracted a particular crowd to the establishment. It's not dinner, it's an experience. People who date (or marry) creatives deserve a lot of credit for dealing with this, and understanding our perspective. Not everyone can appreciate these details, but not everyone cares about them either.

That same restaurant outing can fill a creative's mind with countless solutions to a problem she's trying to solve. The waiter's accent, the copy on the menu, the conversation with her date—all are potential fuel for a grand idea that will change everything. And this is why we all need to leave our homes (and offices) more frequently and live life.

It's embarrassing how often I've stopped a convo just so I could quickly write down something somebody said. My friends have started making uncomfortable jokes about stealing my notebook and reading what's inside. They act like I'm a spy.

 In a perfect world, I'd like to be able to do things off the clock that are as interesting as what I do on it. Since I don't live in that magical unicorn place, I'm left to interject bits and pieces of my day job where I can. This generally results in me art-directing selfies of friends.

 This is not an exaggeration. Bill has, more than once, compulsively art-redirected pitches of mine that I only asked him to read in passing.

"THERE ARE NO SEPARATE SYSTEMS. THE WORLD IS A CONTINUUM."

DONELLA H. MEADOWS

8.

Does your main creative focus inform the rest of your life?

Once a creative, always a creative.

Yeah, definitely. Going back to Darryl's answer in the last question, I see work everywhere. I stop at food aisles and look at packaging. I judge books by their covers (and people by their books on the train), then feel bad about this and invent plausible stories that make me sympathetic to their tastes. "That chick with the trashy romance novel? She has a hilarious romance novel podcast that she runs by night after her day job is over. She gives no fucks what you think of her. Apart from corset-rippers, her favorites are dinosaur erotica, but she avoids bringing those on the train." Also, dinosaur erotica is a real thing. (Look it up). I take pictures of ads on the street and notice when they change. I stop to read them and wonder who they're talking to.

I'd even go so far as to say that there isn't a huge difference between who I am inside and outside of work. My work is with me all the time, in the sense that I feel I'm constantly feeding it when out in the world.

 Once a creative, always a creative. I see the world as a giant exhibit, and like Angela, am continually, constantly observing, ideating, and learning. I like to analyze everything I see. Why that font? Why is he wearing those pants? What is making this person happy/sad/mad? What are people paying attention to?

As Darryl notes, we notice everything. The sound of a commercial. The theme. The customer service. It's hard to turn off the inner critic because, outside the office, we become the end user and experts—roles our clients and their customers normally play.

"I DON'T KNOW IF I HAVE A CONNECTION TO SOME OF THOSE THINGS THAT I SING ABOUT, OR NOT. I DON'T KNOW IF IT'S FORCED OR IF IT'S TRULY INSPIRED BY SOME MUSE, OR GHOST. THE TRUTH IS PROBABLY SOMEWHERE IN BETWEEN. YOU PURSUE THINGS THAT ARE AROUND YOU."

FRANK BLACK

9.

How do you manage money?

Living below your

means buys

you freedom.

49

Get good with money. When we get into more money than we're used to, we have this weird tendency to immediately try tying it up: We decide we need a bigger apartment or a house, or maybe we buy a really expensive handbag.

We also have no pain associated with its misuse. The best thing I ever did was switch to a debit card so I can see the money drain from my life MONTHLY. But that points to a bigger issue: Creatives and money. Not all of us handle it well.

I make crazy buys sometimes, and haven't regretted all of them. But I beg you to set aside just a small percentage of all your earnings, religiously—start with 10%, or even 5%. Put it somewhere you won't touch it. Forget it exists. Doing this will make it easier to steer your life into better waters when shit gets gross. If you want to change trajectories but sit on a beach for three months first, you can do that. If your boss has suddenly gone bananas and is making your life hell, you don't have to need him; you can go.

I feel like I can be pretty fancy-free if shit goes sideways because I'm not relying on anybody's check day-to-day, and the only debt I have left is school debt, which is small and manageable. It didn't always used to be this way, and it makes a big difference. If I have a religion, it is probably that.

 Geez, I can't believe how long it took me to learn this lesson. With every raise in pay, I purchased a bigger house, more furniture, nicer cars. And none of it brought happiness. Living within your means buys you a stress-free existence. Living below your means buys you freedom. I (now) choose freedom.

"FUCK YOU. PAY ME."

RAY LIOTTA • GOODFELLAS

10.

What do you do when your head gets in the way?

Get on with it.

My head is usually in the way. It's in the way right now. Work past it. Muses are fickle and promiscuous; don't wait for them.

Just kidding. All of that is easy to say, but when something is working my brain I can't really focus on anything else until I've sorted it. So within what's possible, I try to handle it so I can focus on my work. If I can't, I "queue" it: Literally add it, and all my confusing roiling thoughts, to a to-do list so I feel a kind of closure that lets me pass to something else. (Seriously. My to-do has included items like "Finish fight with R," complete with little notes about the major points I want to get across.)

 Owing to the procrastination side of things, I don't necessarily wait for muses as much as hope there won't be negative influences around interrupting my focus.

 I have a weird ability to compartmentalize things in my brain. I think it comes from having kids, and learning to tune things out. Parents can hear a crying baby, and know when to tune it out. If you've never had kids, the same sound can be like a drill to the skull. For some reason I've always been able to do the same thing with personal problems, politics, and other distractions. Push them to the side, and get on with the task at hand.

"MY ACTING IS INTUITIVE. I'M NOT AN ACTOR THAT WORKS FROM A HEADSPACE AT ALL. I STAY OUT OF MY HEAD. I DON'T WORK FROM MY HEAD, I WORK FROM MY HEART. I WORK FROM MY GUT."

LAURENCE FISHBURNE

"WHEN YOU HIT A WALL – OF YOUR OWN IMAGINED LIMITATIONS – JUST KICK IT IN."   **SAM SHEPARD**

11.

Do you give a fuck?

I do my best

to give a fuck

about things that

matter in life:

work and love.

Apathy robs. Passion elevates.

When you surround yourself with or immerse yourself in a situation with people as driven or creative as you, it elevates you. When you do not, it robs you. There's nothing like feeding off the positive energy of others. They're the ones asking, "What if...?" Negative people say "We can't."

People often say life's too short to work with assholes. While true, I'd also add that life's too short to spend time with people who zap our energy, yet we do.

Get rid of them or get yourself out of that situation. Call it cancer, call it whatever you want, but when negativity spreads and becomes ingrained in the culture surrounding you, it's over. No matter how resilient you are, eventually you get tired of pushing that proverbial dead body up the hill. When you work with people who make you go "Damn, wish I thought of that!" it makes you want to do better, and in turn, you become better.

Like John Lennon and Paul McCartney! They were best when together, competing as much as collaborating.

That may have been more a yin and yang situation, but that's definitely a case of $1 + 1 = 3$. Paul was the more pop-centric of the two while John was deeper. I don't know that either achieved the same chemistry post-Beatles. There aren't enough metaphors in my golf bag to keep stating this point, but when you're dialed in and surrounding yourself with dynamic people, no other situation will be as satisfying. They push you, and you them. That's when the great happens.

 When shit gets zany, I like to take a step back and remind myself we're not curing cancer. But I'm having high-stress conversations about inane things like the alarming image quality on a client's Twitter page because I truly believe what we do is important. What we consume when we're bored or not thinking is important! Watching the ads of different countries is a masterclass in their fears, phobias, and values.

Like any other industry, advertising needs people who care about it. I have strong feelings about the stuff I consume and the way I live, and I hope the minds that engineered these behaviors in me cared. I hope they were benign.

How creepy. It just occurred to me that a lot of people hope this same thing about God.

Sometimes I give a fuck. Many times I don't. I believe that happiness is understanding when to care, and when to let it slide off to the side. I give a fuck about my coworkers. My colleagues. I give a fuck about my work. And clients. I give a fuck about the world. Ethics. People. Things I don't give a fuck about? Money. Politics. Getting credit. Awards. How popular I am on social media. I do my best to give a fuck about the things that matter in life, work and love.

 I love that Plaid/Humongo kept their awards on display in the bathroom. It's not that awards don't matter, but rather, they didn't rule their lives.

"PASSION IS ONE GREAT FORCE THAT UNLEASHES CREATIVITY, BECAUSE IF YOU'RE PASSIONATE ABOUT SOMETHING, THEN YOU'RE MORE WILLING TO TAKE RISKS."

YO-YO MA

12.
What about boredom?

Let your

mind wander.

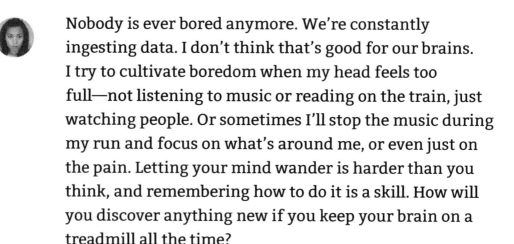 Nobody is ever bored anymore. We're constantly ingesting data. I don't think that's good for our brains. I try to cultivate boredom when my head feels too full—not listening to music or reading on the train, just watching people. Or sometimes I'll stop the music during my run and focus on what's around me, or even just on the pain. Letting your mind wander is harder than you think, and remembering how to do it is a skill. How will you discover anything new if you keep your brain on a treadmill all the time?

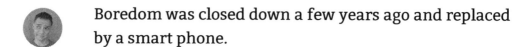 Boredom was closed down a few years ago and replaced by a smart phone.

From an individual POV, we may have more entertainment choices than ever, but in an agency setting? It's very much alive. It exists where leadership keeps taking on mundane work from mundane clients, simply because it's a steady revenue stream.

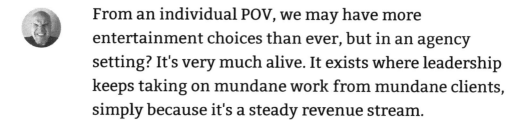 Oh yeah, that boredom is alive and well at agencies across the land. We need to stop the evil that's fostering this climate, for sure.

"BEWARE OF BLUE SKIES AND OPEN HORIZONS."

MICHAEL HASTINGS

13.

What's your take on Mad Men?

The presence

of misery.

I love Mad Men as a concept.

So much of it revolves around that solitary man or team, stuck late in the office, drinking or smoking, trying to poo out an idea but feeling totally constipated. Their misery is part of the show's—and the industry's—glamour. But when you're in that situation, and that misery is present and real, there's nothing sexy about it. It's frustrating, exhausting and abject. We all have nights like that sometimes, but it shouldn't be a regular thing or some awesome state to shoot for.

The great irony of Mad Men is that I think it tried to depict these people, in this universe, honestly: Their inexplicable life choices, their ambiguous emotional responses to things that happened to them, good or bad; their work-related lashings-out at family, or family-related explosions at work. It was sardonic and ambivalent about the happiness its characters were trying to sell, and underscored the unhappiness that ironically drove them. But for some weird reason, people—even ad people—still find that sexy.

The job we do eats your life; if you aren't careful, you will literally slay whole values and long strings of loved ones on the altars of cereal jingles and Budweiser Twitter promos. That's not a rational ambition; that's fucking weird and sad.

I also dislike the modern stereotype that we're all hipsterfolk with zany glasses and well-kept beards. The long-timers I know aren't characterized thus; they're naturally curious, childlike people, and they come in all kinds. They stand out because see beauty and potential in ordinary things; that's what they're trained to do, and who they are. And they manage to stick it out not because they still listen to vinyl but because they're often relativists, not tortured artists staring through the haze of their own cigarette smoke. No one makes sexy shows about relativists.

 I could care less. The more TV I watch, the more annoyed I get by the importance people place on it. It was a fun show for a while. For me, that ended. Who cares?

 It was a glorified Smithsonian exhibit held up by the current advertising industry as the standard for agency life. Forget the myriad "isms" on display (sexism, racism et al.), this show is sweet revisionist history for people who want to remember what they perceive to be the golden age of advertising.

The one thing missed in all takes on the ad business is the team camaraderie and humor necessary to surviving those late nights. The quintessential series or show on the ad industry has yet to be made, but it definitely wasn't Mad Men. It sure had nice art direction on the props, though.

 Yeah. I watched it in HD.

"IS THIS A SUBSTANCE
MUCH LIKE BULLSHIT?"

DON DRAPER

14.

Who's more important—the creator or the curator?

Why not both.

Aren't we both at one point or another? Do we have to make one king?

 No, we don't. It's just that these seem to be the sides chosen. There's also a third perspective: the viewer who is neither, content with being a spectator only. That can get lost at times, especially when we're made to feel obligated to participate in social media. For many, to be thought of as a just causual observer is the worst thing to have happen, as if you offer no value. This is primarily a characteristic of a social media universe consumed by their follow count more than anything. The implications though also extend to creativity. Take the case of:

1. The artist who creates.
2. The critic who judges.
3. The viewer who experiences.

Although No. 2 and No. 3 are often one and the same.

 I think we all get to be artist, critic and spectator at different points in our lives. Creativity needs all three: you spectate to be inspired, critique to develop your own view, and, with the sum, you create. Maybe we valorize creators most because it's in creating that we feel we're finally extending ourselves beyond our vessels.

But sharers also have a crucial role in the game: They determine what rises into the cultural consciousness, and what's lost. The experiencers imbibe what's been made and shared; it becomes part of them, and they go off and sprinkle little pieces of that into the world.

One thing marketers forget is that people are dynamic. They don't like to be buckled down into one box, and they shouldn't be. It's a reason why YouTube vlogger and blogger fame took old media by surprise: When you look at people as passive audiences and not potential makers, you don't realize that scale can tip, and you won't know how to handle it. You'll treat it as a temporary glitch in the system, and slip into obsolescence. But companies who valorize groundswell creators see things differently: Any consuming member of the audience could be the next great creator or contender or media.

 Of course the Creator is more important. (Capitalizing the word on purpose.) Throughout human history, it's the creators who have changed our world. I'd say we need to be concerned about the destroyers. Those dudes ruin everything—creating wars, spreading evil, producing PowerPoint decks and "proven processes."

I look at sharers as creators, too. Not all sharers are as important as others, just as some fine artists are more relevant than their peers. And there are dumpster loads of crap being produced. More than ever in communication's history. I think we'll look back on this era a decade from now and laugh at the kind of sharing people are doing.

One of the many things that moving out of the U.S. has taught me is how narcissistic we Americans are compared to other parts of the world. Moving to Berlin, where social media has yet to be as widely adopted, helped me realize the utter ridiculousness of the selfie. People really don't take them here. And it's wonderful to be able to stand at an epic scene surrounded by people who are enjoying the moment for what it is, rather than doing their best to brag to friends who aren't there. There's a magical collective energy in the air when a crowd is enjoying a moment, and it's completely lost when people lock themselves in their social media force fields.

"WE ARE OUR STORIES. WE TELL
THEM TO STAY ALIVE OR KEEP ALIVE
THOSE WHO ONLY LIVE NOW IN
THE TELLING. THAT'S HOW IT SEEMS
TO ME, BEING ALIVE FOR A LITTLE
WHILE, THE TELLER AND THE TOLD."

NIALL WILLIAMS

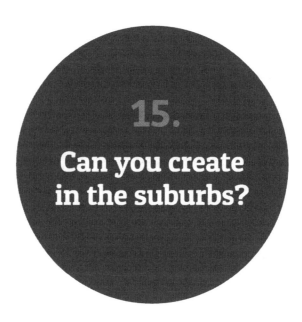

15.

**Can you create
in the suburbs?**

It's location discrimination.

A short, inconclusive and mysterious list of electronic bands from the 'burbs of Paris (specifically Versailles): Air, Phoenix, Daft Punk. What the hell is going on in Versailles, man? We don't look at the 'burbs closely enough. They've got their own secret culture, like squirrels.

 They're filled with creativity. What they need are full-scale production budgets. It seems that most suburban agencies are plagued with local clients who can't spend enough, aren't sophisticated enough, pay poorly, and end up producing lame agencies as a result. There's an issue of "location discrimination" where big brands feel they need talent from the city instead of the agency down the street. That's a shame. I've run agencies in the suburbs of Connecticut as well as New York City—and both were bursting at the seams with creative talent.

My question is why do creative people live in the suburbs? I raised two kids in white-picket-fence-land, and while that was an awesome experience, I don't understand why kidless young people stay there. Too many people never leave the place they're born in, or travel outside of their home state. I want to weep when I meet people who complain about where they live, then do nothing about it. While I implore brands to look locally in their agency searches, I beg creative people to get out. I'm hypocritical like that.

 Creative people live in the 'burbs because, well, money!

 A charming, creative and nomadic friend once said, "We all like to be bourgeois, it's comfortable." There are aspects of the 'burbs that are hard to resist: You can get a big space filled with creative doodads, a garden filled with shrubs, and trees trimmed to look like characters from Spaceballs.

But then again, you're in the 'burbs—too far to randomly run into the creative happenings that sprout up all over a big city. Maybe to be creative in the 'burbs you have to have been trapped there at outset, forced to look at your space creatively before busting out of it. Which might explain why there are so many freaking films about Orange County.

 To this, I say see my answer to question #9 about money management.

 I was the suburban 2.5 kids creative dude. I needed to move to a vital agency epicenter. Lifestyle may be a huge factor in helping you decide where to live, but don't make your career decisions based on convenience if the place you're at isn't worth it. That said, a lot of smaller cities have robust creative environments. Darryl was able to pull a rabbit out of a hat in Danbury, CT, of all places. (Those are my stomping grounds, so save the hate mail.) The point is, it's not always about the location–the people and the agency are what matter.

"YOU HAVE TO LEAVE
THE CITY OF YOUR
COMFORT AND GO INTO
THE WILDERNESS OF
YOUR INTUITION. WHAT
YOU'LL DISCOVER WILL BE
WONDERFUL. WHAT YOU'LL
DISCOVER IS YOURSELF."

ALAN ALDA

16.

Is it possible to grow analog creative in a digital world?

Yes.

No.

Maybe.

Didn't Google do that when it took its best "Search Stories" video from YouTube and put it on TV for the Super Bowl? Different platforms can feed each other, but you have to respect the nature of each platform and the reasons people have for using them. I think it's great when a property like "Crazy Rabbits" can go from video game to cartoon. It expands a universe for fans, gives them one more way to live in it.

That said, I think it sucks when some lazy, condescending suit someplace takes one piece of good creative and hoses it everywhere he can, indiscriminately, just to be there. That isn't multi-platform. That's just basic-bitch broadcast with a new outfit on.

I used to think only data-based creations were susceptible to digital. A few years ago, I learned The Pirate Bay was developing a serious interest in 3D printing because it believes that is the future of pirating. So I guess nothing's safe, not even shoes (or organs!).

We're all bleeding into each other. And maybe that's good; maybe that's just what things do naturally. That's how you make new ecosystems.

 Aside from fine artists, is there no avoiding digital transformation of what it is we create? Everyone loves

Old Spice's social stuff, but it rolled out in print first. Everyone holds Zappos up as a brand that used digital like nobody else, but they ran print ads in the backs of magazines, driving people to their website. Even at its core, analog (the tactile world of print) will always be in the mix. There's a cottage industry for converting digital to analog: sites like Popcanvas.com that let you print your Instagram selfies onto canvas prints. Sexy! Or take 3D printers. That is probably the best example of transforming analog into digital.

Works of art are totally digitized and transformed. There's a whole universe dedicated to Mona Lisa GIFs: http://giphy.com/search/mona-lisa.

Also, there are things like the Human Connectome Project that are basically trying to make us data. People think that once we can nail down our own connectomes (a map of our synapses and neurons), other objects or bodies can use our brains just like we do. Can you imagine the QA process for that? How weird would it be trying to debug the brain of a dead guy?

I hate this question. As soon as anyone suggests to me that anything's "impossible," I make it my personal mission to prove them wrong. Of course it's possible. Everything is possible. Creatives before you have done unimaginable things in every conceivable format. Go forth, break rules.

"DIGITAL FOR STORAGE AND QUICKNESS. ANALOG FOR FATNESS AND WARMTH."

ADRIAN BELEW

"WHEN I LISTEN TO
MUSIC THESE DAYS, AND I HEAR
PRO TOOLS AND DRUMS THAT
SOUND LIKE A MACHINE -
IT KINDA SUCKS THE LIFE
OUT OF MUSIC."

DAVE GROHL

17.

Who's your creative idol?

I don't

like putting

people up

on pedestals.

I'm really jealous of Robin Sloan, who finds a creative way to tell super-inventive stories no matter what platform he's using. The tales combine our tech culture with place, history, and mythology. He's Kickstartered, done presentations where he talks to us as someone from the future, and written books online and on real pages.

I also admire Darryl, who has this open way of looking at a brief that unlocks potential even the brief didn't know it had. And I dig the magic Bill has for taking any situation and transforming it into a horrifically awesome tagline. (He's also artistically spiffed any number of my visually-hopeless presentations.)

Also, I have a thing about Warren Buffett and Jay-Z. And Cindy Gallop for giving no fucks at all and standing up for what she believes in, and Sheryl Sandberg for taking hate on a book that's actually quite honest, balanced and kind, and didn't make me feel like I had a fire being lit under my ass. I want to have a beer with her or whatever it is she drinks; I'm easy, Sheryl. Also, Syd Lawrence from We Make Awesome Sh.it, because he's the kind of developer who makes everything he's doing look like play. It's like everything he codes into the world is a toy he's always wanted. And I can never pick just one Beatle. How can people do that?! Maybe I like Paul McCartney slightly more, though. I don't care what Bill thinks; Paul held that goddamn band together, and he was positive in terrible situations. He would have made an excellent astronaut.

 I don't like putting people up on pedestals. I idolize all the talented people that I've worked with over the years. Like Angela, I am continuously jealous of fantastic storytellers. A friend of mine used to say "Johnny Rotten is the only adult I can look up to." I like that. Although really, I guess I'd ultimately choose Malcolm McClaren over Johnny. And Henry Rollins. Damn, do I feel lazy when I hear about the number of projects that he has invested himself in. He's put himself first, you can tell that he's proud of his work, and he seems to be (from the outside, anyway) happy with his life.

 Not sure I have idols, and certainly none from a creative POV in the business. There are agencies with certain voices whose work I really dig. As for heroes, maybe as a kid, but those were in the arena of sports. Charles Barkley once said (via a WK copywriter I'm sure) that he wasn't there to be a role model for kids. I agree. Once we elevate someone to idol status without first checking with them, we deserve the shattered dreams that follow when they're found with a prostitute in a motel room.

But we can still be inspired by people, and I am: By my

wife Kat and our collective children, by the way Angela writes, which is the way I wish I could write. Anybody reading this who hasn't met Darryl yet will have no idea that he is the most enthusiastic agency owner you could be around.

Kat and I talk about the ultimate party that we would have where we could invite anyone. Whoever would be on that list would start with people who inspired us in some way, from all walks: The arts, politics, tech and entertainment. No social media updates either. Pray you make the invite list.

"I AM FOND OF PIGS. DOGS LOOK UP TO US. CATS LOOK DOWN ON US. PIGS TREAT US AS EQUALS."

WINSTON CHURCHILL.

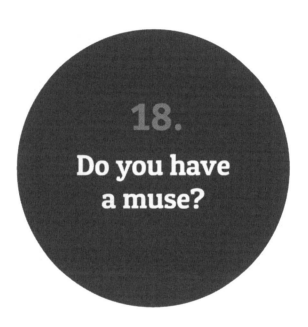

18.

**Do you have
a muse?**

They make for a

good metaphor.

Yes, Kat. In general however, I'd say it's the muse as this collective thing that does it for me, not one person with magical powers sprinkling glitter everywhere and transforming things out of thin air. When we're in the zone on a project and things are flowing perfectly, there are intangibles present that I alone couldn't harness to make it all work.

Are we, in the sum of our parts, greater than the whole territory... or just sum of all our fears? Not sure. What are the specific factors and influences that make **it** happen? Of course talent has to be involved, but a bigger part of it has to do with chemistry and an absence of negativity. When it all works, it's because these things were not mutually exclusive.

 I sometimes do my best work when I've been mulling over something I'm really upset about and haven't slept for days. So I like it when that muse visits, but I would not like to have weeks like that all the time.

I don't believe in muses; they make for good metaphor, but that's all. I'm trying to develop systems that make it easier to do good work, even when I don't feel like it. The most effective ones so far have been carrying a notebook around, and using my dictation app. You look like a jerk when you're dictating though, so I usually pretend I'm on the phone.

 I've never understood the "muse" thing. I'm confused, but inspired by people who claim to have muses, or attribute great work to them. I'm inspired by everyday life, and everything in life—from the broken TV on the street corner, to the conversation I'm having on Skype at the moment. Life is filled with interesting moments, visuals and perspectives, all of which could (and do) lead to brilliance.

Every once in awhile.

 Indeed. To be inspired by life is the thing. We train students to research their client... and how many actually go into a store and watch, vs. just Googling? Watch people. Watch life. Listen with all your senses. Get rid of your TV.

 I like my TV.

"MOST PEOPLE WAIT FOR THE MUSE TO TURN UP. THAT'S TERRIBLY UNRELIABLE. I HAVE TO SIT DOWN AND PURSUE THE MUSE BY ATTEMPTING TO WORK."
NICK CAVE

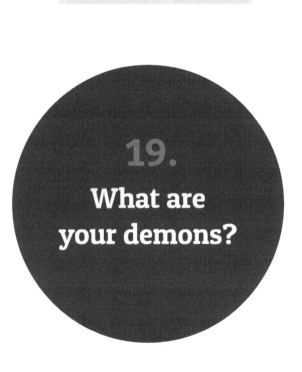

19.

**What are
your demons?**

My demons

are my own.

When I was little, my dad told me that people who make mistakes are people who failed to think. He was always telling me to think, think, think. It was terrifying (and mentally paralyzing. Irony!).

So that's one of my demons: I take it really hard when I make a mistake. I spend hours going back on what I how I could have approached things more carefully, or just differently.

Another one of my demons: I have fought forever with the idea I might fundamentally be a bad person. I think I spend my entire life compensating for this suspicion, and even then, after meeting someone for the first time, I still wonder if I came off as seedy, creepy or bad-intentioned. So I spend a lot of time trying to adjust for these things or work them down.

 Dear reader: Meeting Angela for the first time, she was not seedy. She was super spy-chic, dressed in red, reserved and quiet, sizing up the moment as to whether she could pass off the flashcard of state secrets to me, or vanish in a flurry of midtown Manhattan traffic, never again to be seen in person.

 You offered me orange Tic-Tacs several times. I will never forget how you sat across from me and, after a long pause, tapped your Tic-Tac box on the table and said, "You can have one of these..."

But thank you. I was so excited to meet you. You really are like a bear.

 Facebook. I hate the amount of time I spend there. I'm convinced that part of this is because I've left the country, and I miss my friends and elements of the U.S. I've constantly got the tab open, and it fills every available minute of blank space. That's bad. Blank space and thinking time should be encouraged, celebrated and molded into extraordinary ideas. It's too easy to click and spend a few minutes on Facebook, and I know I've crossed the line where it gets in the way of creation.

 My demons remain my own, as do all of ours. Some of us assimilate them better than others and make great money off of them! For a long time, my challenge was similar to Darryl's in that social consumed me. I was writing Make The Logo Bigger at a clip of five or six posts a day, freelancing, podcasting, keeping up on a job hunt, etc. The one thing I left off the equation was having a life.

20.

What clothes or totems make you feel creative?

Be yourself.

I am a pretty low-maintenance human. It's become really important for me to be comfortable in whatever I'm wearing, especially in a pitch or for travel. Nothing should feel bulky or strained or make me worry about wardrobe malfunctions.

About a year ago I decided to adopt a navy blue uniform on weekdays. It makes it easier to get dressed and I can't think of many everyday contexts where navy blue is screamy or out-of-place. Weirdly, doing this makes me feel more like I'm moving around in the world like less of an object, and that frees up a lot of headspace. It's surprising how much energy worrying about clothes takes up. Fall colors? New boots? Fuck that.

My jewelry is generally always silver, shoes always either blue or black, and nail polish: Nothing at all or semi-permanents, which last for weeks without chipping so I can focus on work. (I wore black polish once to Nestlé and it chipped, and the client made an awkward remark, and it burns my cheeks to this goddamn day.) Everything is pretty much geared to ensuring I don't have to think too much about it and can focus on other stuff.

Totems-wise: I pretty exclusively handwrite with a maroon Sheaffer fountain pen that's kind to lefties. Picking it up is like coming home. Also, and I noticed this recently: Never at any office job I've had have I decorated my desk. This is sad. But it is also what I'm like, I guess. I do envy whimsical desks.

Running an agency in Soho, NYC helped me see style in a new way. I've never asked employees to dress up for a client or presentation, and have regretted it when former bosses expected me to. Wearing a suit and tie in our business is subscribing to a barbaric set of rules. Clients love working with creative people. For many, we are the brightest spot in their day. So if you arrive to client headquarters dressed just like the client, you don't instill confidence or creativity.

People want their lawyers to wear smart suits. And their creatives to dress creatively.

At Mash+Studio, the last agency I ran, we had a habit of never dressing up for any client. Our team showed up to pitches in old t-shirts, shorts and whatever felt right for the day. And we won. Pitch after pitch, client after client. I've worn the worst t-shirts to see some of the biggest, most luxurious brands in the world.

There was a moment, right before I left, when we pitched Hermès, one of the world's most luxurious, buttoned-up, fashionable brands. From Paris. There was some discussion about how we should present ourselves. Do our normal rules apply? Should we dress up for Hermès? This is **Hermès** we're talking about.

We decided to be ourselves. I arrived in an old t-shirt and jeans, as did others on my team, and co-creative Greg came in shorts and boat shoes. We were ushered into a most elegant conference room and served water in a crystal glass more expensive than my shoes. Then we were greeted by the President of the company, in a suit that I am certain cost more than my first home. They looked absolutely fabulous. We looked like we were on our way to drink beer at a Lower East Side dive bar. And we killed it. They loved us. They loved our work. We loved them. We all wanted to work together. At that moment, I realized more than ever that clients are buying talent, personality and brand. We delivered on all three.

Had we tried to dress up for Hermès, there's not a chance in hell that anyone on our team would have been comfortable. How can you outdress the President of Hermès? You can't. They were perfectly dressed for Hermès, and we were perfectly dressed for Mash+Studio. In a way, dressing as ourselves leveled the playing field, because everyone was comfortable. Being yourself always wins. (Later, we celebrated with beer at a Lower East Side dive bar.)

Fun fact: You said "Hermès" six times. You must've liked those guys a lot.

 They were really cool.

 Music. Music. Music. And impromptu lunches with the team. Oh, you need more? 'Righty then. Seconding Darryl's thoughts and Angela's requirements, people should wear underwear to pitches if they feel it helps them, and to Darryl's point, if your agency can't win business the way it normally lives and breathes, it might have lost a little of itself along the way. Win it the way you live it.

 I am so bad at music. I've been listening to the same 80 songs for the last 15 years.

"PEOPLE PAY MONEY TO SEE OTHERS
BELIEVE IN THEMSELVES."
KIM GORDON

21.

Are there any places that make you feel especially creative?

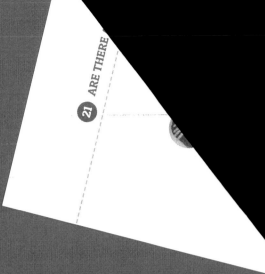

21 ARE THERE

Anywhere

but yesterday.

I have special places I'm in the habit of going to, and tend to stick to them. One thing I like to do is have lunch alone at a restaurant that's not too far, but that people at work aren't in the habit of frequenting. It gives me time to think quietly and come back ready for the next challenge.

I also have dinner by myself at a restaurant near home and just spend hours writing. When I work at home, I feel best at the kitchen table. And I write a lot at beaches. I would like to work full-time in front of a beach someday.

Yes. Anyplace that's different than the place I was yesterday. I've done some of my best work in hotel lobbies, by a pool, in a coffee shop, in the back of a van driving across the country. Changing your space frequently keeps you fresh and full of ideas.

Anywhere with visible horizons. Second to that: wide-open skies. This brings up the idea of views and windows, and why agencies insist on refusing creatives windows while giving the account teams the best views.

As if creative people would be distracted with a view. Really? It would actually inspire because you tend to look away from your monitor, and when not concentrating on the work directly, potential solutions appear. It's the

same thing that happens when I get up and go get a drink
or take a break: I put my mind somewhere else, which
takes the pressure off having to come up with an answer.

"YOU NEED TO GO BACK AND READ THE BUKOWSKI
POEM ON PAGE 28. SERIOUSLY."

ALL OF US

22.

What is all this for?

Leave more good than bad.

I was hanging out with Darryl one time and asked him a question that was bothering me at the time: "Do you feel the need to leave something to the world?"

He thought and said, "No. But I feel the need to give something to the people around me while I'm here."

It was such a relief to hear that. It was like, "Maybe that's enough, and that's okay." It liberated me from this very American idea that we have to be great, leave a crater-sized dent in the world. Maybe we can just take care of people and ourselves.

Sometimes I also feel like that's what we do when we make good advertising, or engage in any creative pursuit: We're sending our little boats out into the dark, hoping to touch someone. And succeeding in that small act can justify a whole life.

 Getting diagnosed with incurable cancer has put me in a position where I've considered this greatly. I'm here to be a force for good. Loads of introspection and reflection have prepared me to be at peace with an eventual death, and an overall feeling of being fulfilled. To Angela's point, I believe that I'm here to build a rewarding life for myself and impact the people that I come in contact with, along the way. Greg Privett, a former coworker of mine, once anointed me with the "A Force for Good" title, and I've since adopted it as my personal mission statement. Nice guys don't have to finish last, even if they die first.

 MOMENT OF ZEN in 3... 2... I've thought about this going all the way back to college, alone in the studio, wondering what purpose life has, not just for creative people, but anyone. Are we killing time or is there something bigger we're a part of? Even if we're killing time in our day jobs, maybe the goal is to leave more good than bad. I may not get there, but I'm still trying every single day to get that part of the equation right.

 Fuuuuck, Darryl pulled the cancer card. How do you even beat that? In other news, he is totally a force for good though.

"WE HAVE THESE AMBITIONS THAT ARE VERY HARD TO ACCOMPLISH BECAUSE LIFE PUTS US IN OUR PLACE. WE HAVE THIS BATTLE WITH MEDIOCRITY."

ALEJANDRO GONZÁLEZ IÑÁRRITU

creativity i

n business

23.

Do you feel like working in advertising is selling out?

You have to sell out to cash in.

At what point do we sell out? Is anything we do for a living always going to be viewed as selling out simply because we're paid for it? Or is it survival? When asked about commercial success versus starving, director Jason Reitman recounts his musician friend's succinct response: "It's really hard to buy a mansion with indie cred."

Susan Sarandon's character Annie Savoy in *Bull Durham* said that the world is a difficult place for those cursed with self-awareness. It's those types who'd say yes to this question. The rest of the industry who view work as simply a means to an end between Tweetups and hot yoga class could care less. As long as they keep the ad industry shoehorned into their lives between the hours of 9-5, it's a matter of providing a service for someone willing to pay for it. I'll let you fill in other professions that fit that same bill.

My college boyfriend liked to say "You have to sell out to cash in." I also recall something Maurice Lévy said at MIP in 2014: TV and film producers are "in show business; we're in the ad business. We respect what they do, I hope that they respect what we do... because a lot of them are coming from our world. It's where they were trained and educated. It was training paid for by advertisers." He looks at respecting advertising as a pay-it-forward.

I think it's awful for fans to impose some idea of bohemian, poverty-ridden purity on artists they love, and worse for artists to impose it on themselves. But we should also be mindful of the kinds of deals we accept, because we're not just representing ourselves; we're representing the fans who see those brands as a shorthand for who they are. We have to respect that.

 There's a lot of confusion about the line between art and advertising. Plenty of people in our industry want to be rock stars, fine artists, and create work on their own terms. That's not the business that we're in. And that's okay. Just because creative people and artists have similar passions and personality types doesn't mean that they perform the same jobs. They don't. And that's okay. People who say that advertising is selling out don't understand the difference between the business models of a fine artist or ad agency.

"THERE ARE TWO KINDS OF ARTISTS LEFT: THOSE WHO ENDORSE PEPSI AND THOSE WHO SIMPLY WON'T."
ANNIE LENNOX

24.

How do you keep current?

Create for a

world you

participate in.

There's so much to keep up with now! I try to strike a balance but inevitably end up feeling like I missed something, and I don't want to spend all my time playing catch-up because I also want to discover new things on my terms, not Twitter's.

In the end, maybe it's more important to be distantly observant of what the industry's buzzing about, to understand how it's changing and why, but focus more on keeping up with the things that pique your own curiosity. That's where the meat comes from; trends are just tools.

 This seems like common sense, but I'm always surprised at people who don't keep up. I know agency owners who aren't on Facebook. Never gave Twitter a shot. How can you expect to produce and create for a world that you're not participating in? Even if you're not using the tools, producing in the media, it is paramount that you understand the impact of these trends, languages, tools and ideas on our society. Otherwise, you end up that old guy writing long copy ads like it's still 1974.

 Wow, the more things change. I've seen the technical divide and it's scary. Those who reach a certain point in this business either make an attempt to understand some of it and how it works, or totally embrace their inner Luddite and eschew progress. I'm not sure we'd be wrong in calling this latter scenario the Singularity's evil twin, the Latency.

Edward Boches once posted about the incoming class he teaches and how he's glad he doesn't have to compete against them. There's something to be said for intangibles found through experience that transcend knowing how to mock up an app you designed. I would turn that around and ask incoming creatives what is it they can learn from senior creatives.

Basing the answer on a technical skillset alone undermines the creative process, because tools alone should not define us, as either practitioners or end-users. If we are truly "collaborative," then all members of the team matter, without personal agendas getting in the way.

"THE ART OF LIFE LIES IN A CONSTANT READJUSTMENT TO OUR SURROUNDINGS."

KAKUZO OKAKURA

25.

What ingredients do you need to start a successful agency?

Leadership.

Love.

Respect.

Love.

A team of talented people who genuinely love and respect each other.

A team of people who are doing what they've always dreamed of doing, in a place that they love. A leader who loves what they do, loves every person on the team, and loves the work that's being produced for the client.

 And I'd add the two things you **don't need**—which are the opposite of that which kills agencies:

Negativity.

Lack of leadership.

Aside from that, I have a mental list of people I would hire to be with me in whatever iteration of an agency we're thinking of, even though I might not have a clue as to what our roles would be. Two of those people are also writing this book.

 Vision. You might not be able to do everything on your own, and your vision may change with the times, but a clear direction is something people can feel. Today it's so hard to be a new agency; a niche gets commodified in a matter of months. You need a firm hand on the wheel, a clear direction, and, conversely, the flexibility to change course, fail fast, correct and optimize.

Assert the culture you want your agency to live. So much of an agency's character, even as it grows, stems from you. Like a child, it inherits your introversion or extroversion, your bad habits, your odd tics. It should also inherit a certain humility and a love of the work. That gets harder as agencies grow bigger, but it really is the soul, and you have to fight to keep it intact.

Lastly, a great leader cares about where his or her people are headed. Nurture their budding skillsets and find out what they want, where the morale level is generally, and whether things are okay at home. When they leave, find out why. Applaud them if they're happy with the choice; learn from them if it was about the environment.

26.

What's more important—chemistry or culture?

Both.

Chemistry. Period. End of story.

You can't have culture if there's no chemistry. Too many agencies confuse one for the other. I've experienced so many different situations within agencies and one thing is clear in this regard: Culture comes from chemistry, not the other way around. You can instill all the culture you want, but without chemistry, your efforts are doomed.

Specifically: Great culture and chemistry are what we're talking about, because one informs the other. When bad chemistry marries bad culture, you know their kids are gonna be messed up for life.

Where situations break down is when bad chemistry is allowed to fester and a fake culture construct is introduced as a band-aid. Good luck with that. If you can't be on the same page with someone, let alone a larger team, introducing a faux finish to the mix—like naming your conference rooms after tropical islands or Disney characters, or having pets in the office—won't matter. Eventually, bad chemistry in the team undermines all other efforts to unite people.

 "You can't have culture if there's no chemistry." I love that you said that.

One and the same. The best pitch team that I ever worked with was at Mash+Studio. We could walk into any room, for any brand in the world, and "present" our work as if we were all at the corner bar, over a beer. Unrehearsed, casual, with lots of back and forth conversation. There was always a sense of confidence, fun, and excitement in the air. Clients pick up on this, and love it. Who doesn't want to work with a team of people who exude fun and love?

 It's infectious.

"THERE IS NOTHING I DISLIKE
MORE IN THE WORLD THAN
PEOPLE WHO CARE MORE
ABOUT IDEOLOGY THAN THEY
DO ABOUT PEOPLE."

JON RONSON

27.

How do you create culture?

True culture is organic and cultivated.

Darryl, Bill and I talk about this a lot. Young agencies often obsess over cultivating a solid culture, and it easily rolls into fanaticism: Creating long and arduous "values" lists that people have to memorize and that are tied to objectives, say.

One well-known French agency is super-focused on its Frenchness. And along with porting all the positive things about "Frenchness" into their work, they embody its negativity in the working environment: After aggressively recruiting great international creatives, for example, they almost actively push them out upon their arrival for failing to be sufficiently "French."

At one agency where I worked, everyone had to justify their bonuses against how they stood up against certain values, like having "one good idea per day." It's a nice thought, but having to justify one good idea per day over the course of three months was paralyzing. It also became an easy way to dock bonuses or make judgment calls about people's "enthusiasm" levels or ability to argue their value.

At another agency it became an obligation to "have fun," and this became a witch hunt where people lost points because they didn't give up enough free nights to take part in dinners or outings. This added stress to teams who worked especially hard and just wanted to be able to go home and spend time with their families.

Bill put it beautifully once on a Skype call: Culture is the fruit of great chemistry, and it's great chemistry that should be cultivated. You can't really make that in a lab.

I'm not saying all of this is for naught. But at some point, when an agency is starting to hit a certain size, I think it's a good idea to sit down with everyone and ask, "What do we value here?" and create a working structure and environment based on those views, loose enough that people can find their own way to them. A culture of play should be built into how people work, not tacked on as a job on top, and a true culture is organic and cultivated with a fine hand, not an iron fist.

I also like cultures that aren't just about the enterprise— at Patagonia or Method Home, people regularly do volunteer work together, like cleaning up beaches, and it sometimes results in a new product idea, like Method's dish soap bottle made of recuperated plastic from the ocean. We need to cultivate cultures that aren't insular and culty, cultures that extend outward instead of inward. That's hard in general, but sometimes it's as easy as saying no to the potential recruit who looks great on paper but has an elitist attitude.

Also: If you need a Culture Officer, I think there's a problem.

It's tough to peg culture creation down to a few "quick easy steps". That's largely because it isn't easy. I guess first and foremost, it starts at the top. The leadership defines culture. Not in a handbook, not on a whiteboard or by "assigning it" to someone.

Culture is defined by how the leaders of an organization behave. How they act in front of employees, clients, in meetings, after work, before work, under stress, after a big win, and in every imaginable situation.

It's also fostered by what leadership allows. Do they exhibit trust in their teams, no matter what? Are they willing to back them up, even if they don't agree? Do they allow their teams freedom to be themselves, to grow, to evolve, to seek inspiration, to push themselves, and to be human? Do they actually, genuinely care about each employee?

Finally, I suppose culture is defined by what the leadership blocks. Do they block bad attitudes, toxic team members, unhealthy and stressful environments, unnecessary work hours, and politics? Do they do it even if it costs money, time, energy and space?

Great leaders create culture largely without thinking about it, or even trying too much. The things that build culture require a mindset that, as a leader, you've either made a part of you, or you haven't. You can't fake culture. I've visited countless companies that point at a foosball table or liquor bar as evidence of "culture." It's not furniture, games, or toys. Culture is the glue that pulls the company together, the fuel that ignites great work and the love that bonds teams to accomplish the impossible.

You can't copy and paste culture from one company to another, or even one office to another. Culture is something to be fostered, grown, supported, invested in, respected, and worshiped.

 And what informs that? The leadership.

This one thing absolutely defines culture and the road map for how things move forward. Start with goodness, and the rest follows. Start with evil, and nations go to war. I also love that Angela mentioned Method, because it tags another dynamic at work here, with a focus away from the person at the top to the entire body of the brand. Tony Hsieh at Zappos, whom Darryl and I met, is someone we found to be employing agency-like methodology in creating that culture, but make no mistake—he has a set path to head down with a clear mandate: Be on it, or be somewhere else. Biz Stone at Twitter had the same focused will when we met him and his team in 2007. Their vibe was less agency and more casual, but no less confident.

That's a slippery slope, because you can pick leaders from any field and come up with pros and cons for each. Could you work for Jobs knowing he inspired as much as he intimidated people?

 I actually go back and forth about the Jobs question. I don't know if I would have stuck it out. At a certain point in my life, definitely, yes. At this point? Less sure. But in Creativity, Inc., Ed Catmull's book on the Pixar ride, he said Jobs evolved as a person and as a leader. I can deal with evolution. Outright consistent tyranny, probably not.

 He would definitely make another great topic to add to our roster. His keynotes are often held up as examples of how to pitch, but the media has basically ignored the real reason Apple is great: His unwillingness to compromise. It's a fine line between tyrant and genius, or is it? Can his determination and singular focus serve as a model for others to emulate?

Jobs had vision, and he fiercely cared about little details that, in the end, do matter, but that people get kinda lazy about—in the same way startups sometimes like to shirk the design bit for "later." I don't think you need to be tyrannous to get your point across, but we also put too much of a burden on "tyranny" as a concept: Is it the Right Way for a leader to behave? Is it the Wrong Way?

It's grayer than that, more loosely-packed and less singular.

Einstein was not a tyrant. He was curious and friendly. But people built bombs with what he did. Elon Musk is pretty tyrannous, but he's also thinking less as an individual and more in the interest of the species.

"THE GREAT LAW OF CULTURE IS:
LET EACH BECOME ALL THAT HE WAS
CREATED CAPABLE OF BEING."

THOMAS CARLYLE

28.

**What makes
a creative
environment?**

Give people

a little...

Christopher Alexander's The Timeless Way of Building is a great study on this question. It basically says that you have to build spaces that intuitively motivate people to create the rituals and behaviors you're hoping for. It made a big comeback among software developers, because they figured out that these principles also apply to UX design.

A space has to facilitate curiosity, collaboration, opportunities to create on the fly, and surprising exchanges. It also needs to be supported by its management, whom people have to trust to not be monitoring their every on-the-book minute. Like Darryl said earlier, you can't just pop a foosball table into a button-up company and expect it to transform into a creative organization.

So basically, naming your office conference rooms is about as en vogue as the '90s theme restaurant craze.

OMG, I had a client whose conference rooms were all named after things that are green: "Fir Tree", "Matcha", "British racing." And one of my more serious clients had conference rooms named after Star Wars planets: Naboo, Endor, Kamino. It's universally always still the same white room with the stale coffee, crumbly cookies and a projector that fucks up.

My worst fave was the pharma shop that used tropical islands. I was the third freelancer shoehorned into the end of an angled desk, in the corner of "Aruba," all three of us staring at a wall. I did not find Aruba at all during my stint there. I doubt the Powers That Be in that company ever did, either. But I did meet a very Zen-like Dude named Jeff. He was into Kung Fu and yoga, but the super aerobic kind of yoga; not the hot sweaty yoga kind. He was a mellow and fast dude, that dude.

I've toured agencies all over the world, and I've noticed that management loves to show off their foosball table, their beanbag chairs, and their beer taps. They all act as if they're the only agency in the world where employees drink beer. And the majority of these agencies are shitty places to work, who don't value their employees, don't fight for great ideas, and don't foster true creative environments. Fuck your foosball table.

Make your workspace fun, give employees loads of space to move around, and then let them at it. Join them at the pinball machine. Encourage them to use goof off space. If you build it and support it, it'll work. Nothing kills a creative space more than management frowning at employees who are hanging out having fun.

29.

How big is the perfect agency?

100+ is

a coin toss.

4 - 12 rocks.
12 - 20 is still great.
20 - 25 isn't horrible.
25 - 50 starts to lose something.
50 - 100 can lose its way.
100+ is a coin toss.

If an agency gets past about 30, it's time to start building teams that operate like little enterprises. People should also be moved from team to team sometimes and have opportunities to interact/share work. More people doesn't have to mean more bureaucracy; it can mean more creative discoveries.

This is a personal question. It all depends on what kind of experience you're looking for. And that goes for both the client and employees. Small, mid-size and large agencies all have their pros and cons. I love small agencies. Like Bill, I believe the agency dynamic changes greatly based on the number of people on board.

Personally, I'm torn. I like working on crews with 5 - 10 employees, but also love a firm in the 12 - 25 range. What's important to me is that the team be small enough to bond as brothers and sisters, but large enough to tackle any size project. A team of 10 or less feels incredibly intimate. A team of 25 allows for specialists, and more diversity of talent. Both are great spaces to play in.

"Big doesn't necessarily mean better. Sunflowers aren't better than violets."

EDNA FERBER

30.

Does collaboration work when it comes to creativity?

When the

stars align.

Of all the things I believe about this business and the act of creativity, the one thing I am unconvinced of most is that collaboration with a group of more than two people in the same room creates a Big Bang/lightning in a bottle idea from nothing.

I'm not against crowdsourcing me some knowledge, but I look to other artistic fields where artists tend to need a place of solace to start. Writers. Painters. Songwriters. Photographers. Graphic designers. Even advertising teams comprised of an art director and writer don't need five other people muddying the waters.

Show me where a group of 8 - 10 people consistently come up with great ideas by meeting and brainstorming.

Lest hatemail start flooding my inbox, I hereby extend an olive branch: Where collaboration can work is in the refinement, implementation and production of said idea. Someone who says "What if..." and builds on that original thought without being the "We tried that already" naysayer? Now you're talking, champ!

Some people get together and it's like the planets aligning. They can share a vision and bring their united strengths to the table like Captain Planet and the Planeteers. Things will always devolve into design by committee when the message isn't clear, people don't really have a reason to be there, someone is dominating the conversation, the goal is vague, or the chemistry is off. You can produce "design by committee" work all by yourself if you're uninspired enough.

Collaboration can work, but only when the stars are aligned. If that makes it seem like a rare opportunity, great. Fantastic collaboration is rare. If the work environment fosters trust, ideation and team building, then collaboration will flourish. But only then. It won't work in a broken environment that rewards politics and "getting credit" over talent and spectacular work.

The other thing that's common in our industry is for brands to put all of their agencies together and have them collaborate on projects. I've been at this table in big agencies, small agencies and with a myriad of clients. It's almost always fraught with politics. The jokes and insults fly seconds after the collaborative conference call ends.

It's sad, because if you think of this from a client's perspective, this should be possible. If it could happen effectively, the work would be rewarded, and everyone wins. I believe that what's missing here is the same issue as a toxic creative environment. If people who are at the table don't have absolute love, trust and respect for each other, they'll never work well together. Maybe clients need to budget for cross-agency off site relationship building. In a warm place with lots of liquor. We'll call them "collaborcations."

 That sounds like Cannes Lions. Can you believe we have a conference that's eight days long?! Of any other industry, we're probably the only one that thinks we're exponentially cleverer as we get drunker.

 But we are exponentially cleverer as we get drunker.

 I take it back. I think the real estate conference is worse.

"POLITENESS IS THE POISON
OF COLLABORATION."

EDWIN LAND

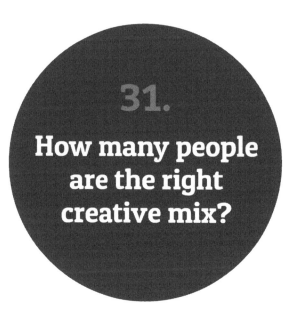

31.

**How many people
are the right
creative mix?**

Two.

Three.

Five.

I hate brainstorms that feel like committees. Everyone just ends up deferring to the loudest or most insistent idea. You literally just sit there and watch the trainwreck happen, and you can't get a word in without being fought down by the loudies.

Otherwise, I feel like the right size for a creative idea really depends. Right now I work with a couple of great teams where the creatives are three or four people. I've tried to combine them but that doesn't work very well. Creative duos are classically great when those people develop a symbiotic system. We have one couple like that at work; they complete each other. In my experience, being in a group of two or three other people has worked the best.

I believe that group size has everything to do with successful ideation. Angela is correct in that they can't be run as committees. There always has to be a creative leader and decision maker in the room.

I think that two people can lead to awkward silence and roadblocks. A team of three people eliminates that issue. Adding another one or two people to the room brings a level of richness and diversity to the thought process, but anything more than that becomes concept-killing.

I never brainstorm with more than five people if possible. Politics and non-participation are invited to the mix the minute you add that sixth person. More than six, and you might as well just hand the job to a kindergarten class.

 I'm in the six range, but whether it's two or eight? They all better be on the same page from a vibe POV. One naysayer will kill it otherwise. We've all been in sessions where two people are the most vocal while the others in the room scribble in their notebooks. Or worse, come to a session having not even read any of the briefing materials first. There is nothing worse than awkward silence.

Having been a victim of many ineffective sessions, resulting in a brainstorm walk of shame back to my desk, I developed a strategy mapping process that distills insights into creative ideas in fairly short order. This isn't an infographic or data visualization popular at tech conferences either. It's a whiteboard braindump that seems like chaos at first but gets separated out into tactics, strategy, insights and user experience by the time things are done. We've also refined the process to be used for client pitches to overwhelming success.

I've actually seen Bill make one of these things and it's cool as fuck. It's like mindmaps before they became creative-hipster-chic and everybody started making software out of them and showing off their doodles at SXSW.

 One of the keys is to let everything in at the outset so that people in the room feels empowered to contribute. The millisecond someone hears the words "We can't" or "We tried that already," they shut down. "What if...?" has always been my mantra in this regard. Don't tell me it can't be done—figure out a way to do it. This is something agencies need to foster in general, not just brainstorms: Are your people positive or negative?

"FEW THINGS IN LIFE ARE LESS EFFICIENT THAN A GROUP OF PEOPLE TRYING TO WRITE A SENTENCE. THE ADVANTAGE OF THIS METHOD IS THAT YOU END UP WITH SOMETHING FOR WHICH YOU WILL NOT BE PERSONALLY BLAMED."

SCOTT ADAMS

32.

Who shouldn't be on a creative team?

Come together, right now.

Domineering people who aggress others, don't listen (you can suss that out when you're talking to them and they keep opening their mouths because they're just waiting to talk), and can't share. I don't care how good they are, they poison the well. Also, people who complain for sport. They demotivate and divide teams. If they were astronauts, they'd literally get their buddies killed in space.

It isn't necessarily my job to come up with the best solution; it's to help my team come up with the best solution, then run with them and support them. Instead of asking me questions, I ask them to come with both the challenge and the solution they're playing with. It saves me time and I can help them work with what they've got on the table. People who only know how to identify problems are energy suckers, and can drive everything to shit if you've only got one problem-solver, and he or she has left the room.

Negative people. I wish these people would all just move to their own town and wallow in misery. Big egos. We're in this together, and I don't care how important you feel you are, need to be, or might be someday. We're all just humans attempting to do something extraordinary. Let's do it and have fun. Together.

Anyone negative for sure has got to go. The runner-up? The Distractor. This would be the well-meaning account or project manager (or other non-creative type) sitting in on the meeting but going about their other work and hitting the keys on their laptop too loudly. Maybe they get up and leave the room during a creative session.

So mean to account people. Did one of them hurt you?

Hardly. It's important that everyone be dialed into the mission or work at hand. Your title or role doesn't matter. Being a hindrance does. Since creatives are generally sensitive to the world around them, they'll notice the one person not contributing in the back of the room. A lack of input can be distracting to others. Apathy kills.

The runner-up to the runner-up? The Side Conversation. It's not that it creates a cacophony, but there are probably some awesome ideas happening between those two people that the rest of the room won't have the benefit of hearing.

Arghhh! I hate that person who leaves the room three times. Everything they're doing is more important than what's going on in the meeting. I agree with Bill—if you can't make time or headspace for the meeting, you don't belong there in the first place.

"A NEW IDEA IS DELICATE. IT CAN BE KILLED BY A SNEER OR A YAWN; IT CAN BE STABBED TO DEATH BY A JOKE OR WORRIED TO DEATH BY A FROWN ON THE RIGHT PERSON'S BROW."

CHARLES BROWER

33.

What do you do when there's just no spark?

Call

friends.

At my old agency we had a thing called Project Smaug: A repository of great ideas we've had that just didn't sell. Smaug has saved us a couple of sleepless nights.

 Pull together your two best friends at the agency. Tell them you're stuck, and you need 45 minutes of their time. Brainstorm, without reviewing a brief, or any details. Something will come of it.

Like Angela, I've also kept a file of "the best ideas in the world." These are legends just waiting to be created. All they need is a client to say "yes" and a budget to be approved. I carry this list with me today, and could pitch them to nearly any brand in the world. Let's go.

 Great Ideas that get rejected by one client are often saved for other clients—if the idea is right for the particular industry.

"The important thing is somehow to begin."

HENRY MOORE

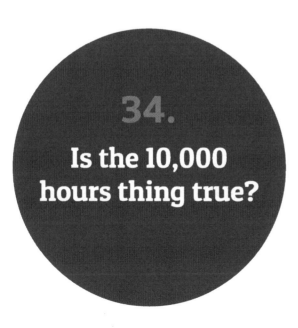

34.

Is the 10,000
hours thing true?

Working harder or working smarter.

Hello nature/nurture, how are you, old friend?

Are we born with talent or can we learn it? Angela posits this as the essence of why we create: Who chose who? Did we always know we were creative or did we learn it? This distinction is often the defining point in our lives when it comes to creativity.

Will 10,000 hours make you an expert at anything? Perhaps; for the craft part of the equation, it's almost a given. And I'd posit right back at ya' that not even time equates to being great in defining the essence of something.

 I go back and forth about this. A lot of business books say it's not about working hard for years, it's about working smart for one year or two. On the one hand, to get really strong at something you need to put in the time—but you need to do it in the right place, working on stuff that challenges you or reinforces things you have to master. If you're just whiling away for 10,000 hours, you're not going to get much further.

 If you are not blessed with the gift of self-awareness, the kind of person who knows who or what you're supposed to be or do in this world, you need to put your 10,000 hours in, because you do have an obligation in this regard, and that obligation is to yourself, first and foremost. No matter how long it takes you to find your purpose, once you know what it is, pursue it with extreme prejudice and without compromise.

There's a recent school of thought that says passion for something can be achieved if you simply apply time against it. So take 10,000 hours, invest in a pursuit, and you will cultivate the interest that generates and regenerates passion for it. I'm not sure how you gain passion for the very thing you knew nothing about previously. It's just not anything I've ever seen done.

When I played and later coached youth sports, I could instruct on ways to be faster, but I could never make someone fast. I could run players through exercises to get their conditioning up but I could not instill will or drive. I coached players with great talent that I wished the Rudy-like players on the rest of the team even had a fraction of.

Otherwise, if simply practicing a thing was the solution, we'd all be amazing at something we spent countless hours repeating. I spent a lot of years practicing bass after school and weekends ... Adam Clayton from U2 didn't.

Even though, years after the band had made it, he went back to take lessons and relearn how to play properly. Regardless, only one of us is in the Rock and Roll Hall of Fame.

You coached youth sports?! That explains so much...

Yelling was kept to a minimum, rest assured.

The older I get, the longer I'm in this business, the more I feel capable of predicting how things will play out. I can see the bad clients. I can feel the right concepts. I know deep inside what will work and what won't. I'm not convinced that we're born with this, and pretty sure I know these things because I've done them all 147 times before.

I first started to notice this when accompanying colleagues who were in their twenties to client meetings. I could see how things were going to unfold, to the amazement of younger coworkers. I wasn't the Nostradamus of advertising; I'd just experienced this exact situation before. Many times before. I could see where my ~~hours~~ years of experience helped me understand the situation in a clear way. I think they call that wisdom, and I believe I've earned a little bit of the wisdom juice.

"TEN THOUSAND HOURS
I'M SO DAMN CLOSE I
CAN TASTE IT."

MACKLEMORE

35.

How many hours are too many hours?

The exploitation of passion.

I went through this trying series of pitches for one big client who took six sleepless months to win. The agency was small, and demands were HUGE. I slept so little that my body would steal sleep: I'd miss my metro stop, sleep through alarms, fall asleep in the bathroom...

It was bad. It made me bitchy, it made us fight. I don't think we were ever worse with each other than we were then. When we won the pitch, I contemplated signing off the project because I didn't want this scary place to be my life. Before making my final decision, I talked to the Creative Director and he was basically like, If you stay, you run the team, so organize the project in a way that people won't kill themselves like that.

That was the right kind of support, and he stood behind it: As long as my team was putting in the work, he didn't stand over us and go, "Why aren't they working more?" We also learned to manage big pitches without going kamikaze every time, and in one of those rare events that hardly ever happens in this industry, I went from being crazy-overworked to being able to decide, and manage my own time in a healthier way. But I probably wouldn't have learned how, and why it mattered, if not for that six months.

An environment that systematically overworks you

won't yield the best work you've ever done, won't make you happy, and won't help you create the relationships you need to pull you through hard times. It's okay once or twice a year, but if that becomes your life, it's shit all around.

That said, I LOVE being in a zone where I'm locked in on a project, really feeling the work, and ready to pour my all into it until it's done, because I'm obsessed and I've forgotten to eat and it doesn't even matter. It doesn't happen often. It's precious. That's a good kind of "too many hours." I think we all have moments like that.

But that passion shouldn't be exploited, and should be carefully measured. Because we're doing creative work with tight deadlines, "too many hours" is something that happens easily and often, and it's valorised by society and a lot of agencies, which is a really dangerous place for us to be in. Young people especially are happy to give their all until they crash, and by then they're in a vicious cycle that they themselves don't know how to stop.

So I try to nip that in the bud before it's a problem—there have been times when I've had to force people to schedule time off, or redistribute work so a few people aren't saddled with long nights or weekend duty. I don't want them to get into the habit, and I don't want to contribute to creating an agency culture that takes advantage of honeymooner zeal.

It's time that leaders really took note here, and took charge. There's a horrific, disturbing trend taking place in young agencies and startups. Young employees are celebrating the fact that they're pulling all nighters, and working the weekends. They've been brainwashed into believing "it's awesome!" and that it's something to be proud of. It isn't. Leaders who foster this environment are irresponsible jackassess, killing their employees an hour at time.

The work has to be done.

But you have a life, too. If work can't be completed on a reasonable schedule, this is a management problem. Sure, there will always be an occasional late night or weekend deadline. Occasional is the key here. When this becomes the rule rather than the exception, it's a sign of a broken organization, and everyone should expect leadership to fix this. A great leader will recognize a job well done—not the number of hours required to produce great work.

I'm appalled at how often you hear agency people brag, "we're soooo busy" or "we've been working day and night for weeks straight," as if this is some measure of success. "Busy" doesn't mean success. Long hours don't bring success. Success comes from talent, first and foremost.

I believe the success of an agency (and great culture) is shown when employees are instead bragging "I'm doing the best work in my life" or "I'm so proud of the project we're working on." It should always be about the work. And as Ben Kunz, a wise friend of mine once said, "Nobody should have to kill themselves to be successful." Amen.

 When a select few take on the majority of the workload for too long, Houston, we have a problem. There's a breakdown in the system somewhere. That's different than having to throw hours at a problem that just won't budge.

As my design professor in college said, "It takes as long as it takes to do it right: four hours, four days or four weeks." There's truth there, depending in no small part on how much Blink/10,000th hour skillset you possess. It's that hard drive we have full of rich experience that allows us to intuit solutions in a given situation and gauge how many hours it will take.

But if the same team is killing it with late nights and

weekends constantly? That's a systemic issue. Perhaps the owner won't address the issue of the few picking up the slack for others on the team. Or maybe the agency's clients are walking all over them and it's allowed because nobody wants to rock the boat. This is usually backed up by the statement, "Hey, they're paying us." When you as a creative can't affect change within the agency, then it's time to affect change within yourself and walk.

 It's okay if your personal success trajectory doesn't match your company's. Anyone who tells you the opposite is a dick.

"NOBODY SHOULD HAVE TO KILL THEMSELVES TO BE SUCCESSFUL."

BEN KUNZ

36.

Is it important to believe in the idea?

If you don't,

don't let it out

of the room.

Yes. Alex Bogusky sold us burgers before selling us something better. It's not necessarily hypocritical behavior. Why shouldn't we consider it is a genuine crisis of one's own faith relative to their work and the impact it has on not only them, but the customer? Eventually, any self-respecting creative should question the moral and ethical dynamics of the work they do and the people they do it for.

But you should stand for something and have a viewpoint. At some point, after a certain age, we transition from being able to have a POV about the work—or defending it to colleagues or presenting it to a nervous client—to deciding what it is you will or won't work on, based on what your moral compass says.

 A good and way-more-successful friend once told me we have to be schizophrenic to make it in this industry, and no one is paying us for our holistic values. I get it: We have to compartmentalize. But I'm one of those people who can't really get on board if I don't get the why of it. I want a strong foundation, but I also want to fall in love. I think clients do, too.

 YES, YES, YES. If you don't believe in the idea, don't let it out of the room. Ever. Never. No way.

"There is nothing worse than a brilliant image of a fuzzy concept."

ANSEL ADAMS

37.

**Who are you
accountable to?**

A work/life, life.

More to clients than I'd like, but I also feel lucky enough to say that, at this point in my career and my life, the buck stops with me. I need to find a way to be okay with what I'm doing.

As a freelancer I have fought against bad ideas and, if we can't agree, both of us can just walk away. As an employee I've fought against bad ideas and been overridden. It's enough then to say my piece and let things play out as they will. Most things we work on are not worth dying for. In most cases I have felt accountable to my team.

When you're reliable, competent at what you do, good to your clients and willing to both learn and teach, there will always be another opportunity around the corner. There has never been a moment in advertising when I ran the risk of starving, and I also think I've finally arrived at a place where I know I can do cool shit while still protecting work/life balance. Nobody should give you shit about it that. (And if they do? Fuck them. They're not Elon Musk. Unless they are. In which case, agh, sucks for you, but also, congratulations! You're probably going to be responsible for the first sustainable human colony on Mars, or at the very least for reducing humanity's reliance on fossil fuels. Pros and cons, **Jesus**.)

I agree with Angela. I want to come home every day proud of the work that I've done, and comfortable with the decisions that I've made or supported. When I can't achieve these things, I do everything in my power to make change. Most of the time, that can be solved without major drama. You can't go quit your job every time the boss is an asshat.

Never underestimate the power of honesty and conversation. People are quick to complain to the wrong people, and while there's some value in venting, it's not going to help the issue at hand. Having an honest conversation with the person who can change what's bothering you will solve the problem the majority of the time. And when it can't... it's time to move past it.

Early in my career I would have said the work, hands down, before family, before anything. Now? It's still the work, but to a lesser degree. Ultimately you are accountable to yourself. If you produce work that you don't feel good about or which leaves you dissatisfied, you have no one else to blame. Clients may pay the bills, but they still count on you to come up with something they couldn't.

38.

What's the creative director's job?

The

compass.

To be a cheerleader, to be passionate. To inspire your team to produce the best work of their lives. To protect great work from being ruined by account people who are terrified of it, clients who don't understand it, and budgets that will squeal under its weight. To bring it all to life in a way that leaves everyone wanting to tell their friends about it. To do all of this—on time, on budget, and with the enthusiasm of a marathon runner crossing the finish line.

 To whip out the compass when ideas and strategies have gotten lost in the weeds. The CD at my old agency was really good at looking at something we tortured ourselves over for weeks and saying things like, "You've got one hour with the client. Which part is she actually looking forward to? Why aren't we building toward that?"

 And to that sage council, I would simply add this: To provide inspiration and confidence to all.

"THE ROLE OF A CREATIVE LEADER IS NOT TO HAVE ALL THE IDEAS; IT'S TO CREATE A CULTURE WHERE EVERYONE CAN HAVE IDEAS AND FEEL THAT THEY'RE VALUED."

KEN ROBINSON

39.

What's the role of an account person on a creative team?

Trust.

Account people can't be order-takers. Sometimes they become part of a system and not part of a team. Account people can shut down bad shit, and at their best, they can be there to protect the creative, like a gallerist for an artist.

Managing expectations, and protecting the creatives. On the client side I try to ensure our work is never undervalued. I also do a lot of listening and try to be proactive about moments when they're likely to get bored or are expecting something big. My job is to show them how our work supports their ambitions, and make my teams look like the geniuses they are.

It's also about knowing how to ask the right questions once the client gives the stream-of-thought version of what they want, because I have to filter that into a brief that isn't scary, too vague, or likely to entrap us when we've produced a recommendation. You can't just serve up what the guy said, unfettered.

I've had creatives just shut down because they didn't get the brief: Either there was too much information or too little, or the constraints weren't clear, or they didn't know who they were supposed to be addressing. It's actually really hard to produce a good brief, but everything hinges on that. I also want to make sure the client has coherently nailed down what they're trying to accomplish so they aren't unpleasantly surprised when the time comes to present. It saves everybody time and ensures everybody's getting what they want.

One more thing: I give the creatives a lot of client context. If they end up working with this client a lot, I want them to understand the mentality and politics as well as I do. Who are they trying to please, what are they into, what are they trying to protect? What pop culture artifacts really win them? They should never be in a lurch if I'm not around, and a good account person shouldn't be stingy with the little things that may be critical to unlocking a yes, even if they're not always used.

 What's the role in real world vs. perfect world? Different animals.

I want to work with smart account teams who aren't nervous, who get the brand, and who understand that creative will get help us all get there. Wherever "there" is. My friend Zeke believes the hardest thing to teach in design is restraint. That applies to everything in an agency. Account teams by and large are inherently different in terms of workflow than creatives, and can have more time on a project to wait for revisions than the design team has to make them.

This creates tension because, sooner rather than later, an account person is going to be asking for a check-in. This will likely come two days earlier than last agreed upon, at which time "concerns" over messaging and layout creep in. Of course they will, because well, um, WE'RE STILL A WORK IN PROGRESS.

That's like judging a band by their soundcheck. This is where restraint comes into play. But restraint by an account person will only happen if there's trust between all. I trust you to give me what is needed so we can make the client look good, and you trust me to deliver on that promise.

"YES, CROWDS CAN BE VERY SMART AND OFTEN IF YOU'RE LOOKING FOR EFFICIENCY CROWDS WILL DELIVER YOU EFFICIENCY. WHAT THEY DON'T DELIVER YOU IS THE BIZARRE AND THEY DON'T DELIVER YOU THE UNEXPECTED OR THE SURPRISING. IN FACT, THEY'RE DESIGNED TO SUPPRESS THAT."

CRAIG MAZIN

40.

What are briefs good for, anyway?

Fuck briefs.

A clear target market, a clear challenge, a clear end goal, a single and shining clear insight. Whatever assets they're currently using—existing slogans, related collateral, tone of voice, what kind of music or pop culture elements the client likes that we could build on or blow out of the water—always help too. It sounds silly, but knowing a guy is really into "House of Cards" can be enough to Trojan Horse a good idea a few crucial steps through the gate.

What's a brief.

Fuck briefs. If you can't summarize the problem in a 15 minute conversation, you've got a bigger issue. I've heard people remark about "how he wrote the best briefs." Really? How is that a judgment on someone's creative ability? People get buried in briefs, and they hold back great ideas. I'm not saying that you should develop work that's off target, but there's no need to dig into the weeds during a brainstorm, either. It's my experience that most people don't really read them anyway, or just skim them 90 seconds before joining the meeting. A great creative director can summarize the problem and lead ideation without a document chocked full of rules.

People won't always remember everything that came out of that CD meeting, especially if they're working on multiple projects at once! At its best, a brief redirects you like a compass when you're halfway through ideation or have gotten sidetracked by something else. I don't think they should be 20 pages long, or that they should somehow define the idea, but I do think knowing how to write a good brief is invaluable.

PERHAPS my initial response was not enough. One thing that I see agencies do all the time is make the brief do too much. There's the brief for the client defining business goals and objectives, and there's the brief the creative team needs, distilling those goals into creative speak. And of course, written with some voice. Why do internal docs at agencies sound so devoid of life? Briefs, as with all agency docs, should inspire—or at least entertain you.

Agreed that briefs shouldn't sound like PRs (and neither should PRs, for that matter). They should start walking creatives down the path of the story, and tone of voice is critical to that.

So maybe it's more about where it's used. I don't think it matters in a brainstorm. It's hindering. But Angela's correct—I can see where it's a useful document to help shape the results of a brainstorm to meet the client's goals. Put it this way—all I want out of a brainstorm is "we're going to put the product on Mars." You don't need a brief to inform that high level concept thinking.

 Unless the client's biggest competitor is Mars, who is killing them in the candy business and has shit tons more brand recognition, which would be handy to include in the brief.

"IF YOU WANT TO BUILD A SHIP,
DON'T DRUM UP PEOPLE TO
COLLECT WOOD AND DON'T
ASSIGN THEM TASKS AND WORK,
BUT RATHER TEACH THEM
TO LONG FOR THE ENDLESS
IMMENSITY OF THE SEA."

ANTOINE DE SAINT-EXUPERY

41.

**How do
you produce
for audiences?**

We are

those people.

There are moments when I'm a really gullible consumer, and others when I'm really skeptical and obsessive. It's important in our line of work to remember we are those people: Consumers at their best and worst. When we forget, that's when we produce stuff that's way out of touch. Steve Jobs wanted to make things he wanted to buy, things that would shut down all his skepticism and just rock well. Steve Jobs used this idea as his compass for producing the iPod: He wanted to make something he wanted to buy, something that would shut down all his skepticism and just rock well.

 Audiences are made of people. They're human. They're not numbers on a Powerpoint slide. It's difficult to sum them up with generalities, yet that's what we all believe: That we need to deliver the perfect strategy, concept or campaign. The more you can identify with your audience personally, the more you'll connect with them. If you're not in the demo, find someone who is. Invite them to the team. Spend time with them. Learn everything you can about them. As creatives, I like to say that we're amateur sociologists. So be a sociologist, and study your target.

 Agreed.

The work that works best has always been something that aligns with things I'm interested in or at least have solid knowledge of. That doesn't mean you have to use your client's product either. I never forget that the audience is the one we do this for, so making sure they get what they came for—or what we created for them—does what it's supposed to.

"I DON'T BELIEVE IN ELITISM. I DON'T THINK THE AUDIENCE IS THIS DUMB PERSON LOWER THAN ME. I AM THE AUDIENCE."
QUENTIN TARANTINO

42.

What do you do when there's not enough money to sustain the idea?

I love this

challenge.

A lot of ideas can still be great when they're pared down; it's harder but a more interesting challenge. You end up taking out a lot of moving parts. But if it's one of those "build me a mansion for the cost of a condo" situations, set the big idea aside for somebody who really deserves it. It doesn't do your idea any favors to undervalue it.

 I love this challenge. It's one we're all familiar with. For most small agency workers, it's a typical Wednesday afternoon. I believe that any idea...any idea...can be scaled and produced in a way to suit almost any budget. And this is where a great Producer really shines. She'll see the possibilities where everyone else sees the impossible. Great producers are the real magicians in our industry.

 I've often found it's not the budget clients lack, but the courage. As Darryl said, a great or even solid idea can scale up or down accordingly because there are always ways to execute it. It's one thing for clients to want to try something different; what's harder to find is the bravery to approve it. Of course, this is the one dynamic that creates the most tension in getting an idea through.

Clients by nature are risk averse, because they live in a well-defined, results-driven world of red and black, sold/didn't sell, shipped/didn't ship. Creatives, on the other hand, are not so easily defined because the creative process itself is not black and white. It's about many possibilities and outcomes, not one. It's this dynamic that creates rifts between brands and agencies.

"IF AT FIRST THE IDEA IS NOT ABSURD, THEN THERE IS NO HOPE FOR IT."

ALBERT EINSTEIN

"HOW DOES A PROJECT GET TO BE A YEAR BEHIND SCHEDULE? ONE DAY AT A TIME." | **FRED BROOKS**

43.

What is wrong with the agency/client relationship?

Parents

and children.

The client is the client. They have stakes, just like us. One of the most helpful things I've learned to do is become aware of the client's stakes: What's their boss like, did the company have a good or a bad quarter, what's going on with the client as a person. If you know their stakes, you can respond in ways they intuitively find relevant.

It also often helps explain their behavior. We used to have a great client who understood the long-term benefits of social media and was really easy to work with. But before she left for a year-long maternity leave, she suddenly became really critical of our work and was calling all the time, demanding we fix this and that, saying the creative wasn't strong enough or reflecting the brand very well.

We were super stressed-out. We didn't know what happened or why she suddenly seemed to hate the work. But by asking around and spending valuable face-time with her, we learned that the company didn't have a replacement for her, so a separate department, the brand department, would be "provisionally" taking over social media. In this company, once somebody "provisionally" takes you over, it's basically a permanent move. That department already had its own agency and wasn't convinced we shared their vision.

Long story short, we realized our client was trying to protect us—to make sure that when the brand people started poking around, we wouldn't be faced with questions she hadn't already forced us to answer. Once we understood that, we knew how to tailor the creative, and we also knew how to adjust our arguments to protect big creative decisions. Things turned out fine with the brand team and I don't take that for granted; we made it through because we took the time to understand the stakes. The people who pay us are very rarely our enemies; they're just people, and if they go bananas on you, there's usually a reason they're so stressed. Find it. Find a way to support what they really want, and you'll do fine. You can even wiggle in change, bit by bit.

 Yes, agencies can respond intuitively, but only if brands let them by valuing them as a partner, and not simply a "vendor." They're real good at saying the former in Ad Age articles but in the real world, the walk they walk is based on the latter. Agencies need brands more than brands need agencies. If anything was broken with today's agency-brand relationship, it's that it's still very much a parent > child relationship. The brand says jump, the agency says "How high?"

The scenario Angela mentions highlights that because we often aren't privy to what goes on behind the scenes.

We need to sit next to this brand person or that one just to catch up on the latest gossip about the very brand we're supposed to know inside and out.

People are afraid to communicate. They're just clients. They're actually human. It's okay to ask them questions. To clarify. To email them animated GIFs. To make a joke. To use a swear word. To admit to a mistake. I think that once everyone stops the high school theater-level drama that we attach to our roles, we can just be ourselves. And that's when the walls come down. My best clients have always been people who evolved into becoming great friends. There's immediate trust, confidence and comfort on both sides of the fence. And I never ever want to let a friend down. If you can find clients who are friend-worthy, you're in the best place possible.

"MAKE FRIENDS WITH YOUR CLIENTS, BUT NEVER GROVEL."

DAVID OGILVY

44.

Have you ever "taken one for the team?"

That is not

your job.

I've been in a few situations where a boss put me in a room because he knew the client or prospect was into me. Sometimes it was nice, like a VP who just happens to really relate to you; but once it was a guy who likes Asian girls, which was just horrible.

This is the kind of crap that all women have to deal with at some point, and because every instance of it can't become a fight, you have to define for yourself what's okay and what's not. I don't mind sitting in for one meeting and exchanging jokes with some weirdo to break ice or whatever, but I also don't want to work for creepers. This isn't goddamn Mad Men.

No matter where you are in your career, you don't have to do anything with anybody who makes you uncomfortable. And don't avoid conflict until you're so upset that you explode all over the place. Don't take any shit—sexist jokes, creepy leers, dinner invitations that alarm you. That is not your job. But it's also critical find the way to not take shit that best suits you, because you can't escalate everything to a sexual harassment lawsuit. That shit freaks people out—and sadly, nobody believes how often women get put in wack positions in their career. If it isn't would-be seducers, it's deranged wannabe father figures projecting all their nonsense onto you, and they're both just as bad.

Beyond that, honestly, an account person's whole job is taking one for the team: Absorbing the client's stress over unmet KPIs, and absorbing the creatives' stress about lacking the flexibility to make what they want. When my team works weekends, I work weekends. When they're there late, I stay late. Nobody likes it, but few things are more demoralizing than feeling taken advantage of by your boss, and it's one of the big morale-biters I can actively help fix—but it also makes it that much more personal when we get to a point where it's like, okay, let's get our shit together, I don't want to lose another weekend staring at the office wall and hating my life.

I haven't entertained clients that I didn't naturally want to spend time with. I'd just rather not hang with you than pretend we like the same things. I think it's wrong for clients to expect to be entertained, and harks back to the 1970s model of business. If you like golf or strip clubs, and I don't—go have fun. Without me. There's nothing gained by awkwardly dragging me along. It's not imperative that we love hanging out together in order for my team to do stellar work for your brand. That said, some of my best friends are former clients. When you do hit it off, it's fantastic.

I took a $5,000 cash advance against my credit card once to give to a client while we were in a Vegas casino. The next move we did on their behalf I felt less sleazy about: Went to Home Depot (while I was at an agency up North) and FedExed a generator to them in Miami ahead of an impending hurricane. Does that count?

"THERE ARE ALL SORTS OF PIMPS. THE FLASHY YOUNG
PIMPS NEVER LAST LONG. THEY DRINK AND GET INTO
FIGHTS AND A FEW YEARS OF THE HAPPY LIFE TURN THEM
INTO CRIPPLED ALCOHOLICS. THERE ARE ALSO CRIMINAL
PIMPS, WHO LAND UP IN JAIL. BUT THE QUIET POWERFUL
PIMP LASTS."

JANWILLEM VAN DE WETERING

45.

When were you financially taken advantage of?

When

weren't we.

Early on, startups I worked with would offer shares in exchange for a lower salary. Surprise! Those shares never materialized. If I ever do that again, there won't be any singing and dancing until the paperwork is on the table.

For freelance work, I charge percentages up-front unless I know the client well. And when I'm working in an agency, I've learned it's just not worth it to have a client who's low-balling you on every aspect of the contract. Contracts are collaborative—both people should feel glad when one is in place—and you shouldn't feel like you're sacrificing the lives and souls of your team just to get a sexy brand on your roster.

In general though, I don't think people look to fuck you over, but sometimes things happen and priorities change. Be clear with the client if the executional demands are putting an unforeseen strain on your resources. In French there's this saying, "let's cut the pear in half"—when you say something, they'll usually meet you halfway, because they don't want to lose you either.

Every hour of every day in the early days of starting my first agency. This turned out to be a valuable lesson, teaching me the value of a fantastic client. Today I have no qualms about asking and expecting to be paid fairly for my talent, experience and work. I've gained the confidence to see through empty promises and people who are just looking to take advantage.

 When wasn't I?

SO YOU DROP ALL YOUR DEFENSES AND
YOU DROP ALL YOUR FEARS
AND YOU TRUST ME COMPLETELY
I'M PERFECT
IN EVERY WAY
CAUSE I MAKE YOU FEEL SO STRONG AND
SO POWERFUL INSIDE
YOU FEEL SO LUCKY
BUT YOUR EGO OBSCURES REALITY
AND YOU NEVER BOTHER TO WONDER WHY
THINGS ARE GOING SO WELL
YOU WANNA KNOW WHY?
CAUSE I'M A LIAR
YEAH I'M A LIAR
I'LL TEAR YOUR MIND OUT
I'LL BURN YOUR SOUL
I'LL TURN YOU INTO ME
I'LL TURN YOU INTO ME
CAUSE I'M A LIAR, A LIAR
A LIAR, A LIAR

HENRY ROLLINS • LIAR

46.

Have you ever been ripped off creatively?

Sometimes, the same idea just happens.

Yeah, I've been ripped off the way strategists sometimes get ripped off: A client asked for a complete strategy, didn't buy it, and used it anyway.

These things happen, and because they altered the creative slightly, there was nothing I or the agency could do (what could we say—that we invented the concept of activating influencers?).

You'll have a moment like that at some point in your career. Let it go. Move onto the next thing and be even more kickass.

Good clients know that when they steal an idea, they're burning a bridge to future ideas and insight from that agency. So if they want to steal, that's fine. People can steal a blueprint; they can't steal your expertise or experience. You can still go on and do amazing stuff.

This is one reason I'm not crazy about doing repeat pitchwork. Some "potential" clients send five or six briefs to work on simultaneously, or brief you once a month, and never buy anything. You can tell they're just mining the crap out of you.

Those ideas aren't free; somebody else is paying for that time. It's a strain on the agency and on some other client who is actually paying the bills. Clients who behave like they've been left unattended in front of a plate of cookies won't nurture an agency relationship well; they will shirk you dry, even if they finally do decide to pay.

 That old adage about it being the ultimate compliment– I've always thought like that. I honestly believe that ideas are dime a dozen. The ability to sell an idea to a client who will support and fund it–that's the magic.

 Dime a dozen is one thing, but it wasn't a compliment when it happened to me twice. In both cases it involved an agency presenting to a brand, and leadership failed to take the necessary precautions to protect the ideas. One was for a cable TV show that we presented to. Our contact, who was a showrunner at the time, reviewed our presentation and reality show outline, but said they couldn't see the concept happen given the prevailing attitude toward our client's industry (alcohol & spirits).

Never heard another word until seven months later when we saw the show we pitched appear magically on E! with the same title (but one word changed). When the agency declined to pursue any action, I was angry. When your own agency doesn't have your back, there's a loss of trust that doesn't come back.

The more recent one involves a music streaming service that sold to Apple and rhymes with Beats. I'll leave it at that.

As for RFPs, they are the worst barometer for how an agency will perform on a given project. Basically, the brand wants planning and concepts—that require research, resources and creative assets—then judge you on whether the price is right. Or they use your agency as a third vendor because they always triple-bid everything.

Worse, the RFP is usually a cobbled-together document from whatever someone on the brand side could Google, or whatever they could find from the last few RFPs they sent out. Over half of the doc is a formality, having nothing to do with what your agency should do. The other half includes the kitchen sink as far as objectives go, many of which contradict something written earlier in the doc. You then spend a week trying to get clarification on things they should have made clear to begin with.

Bitter yet? Hard not to be.

I applaud CurrentTV for trying to shake up the pitch process by opening it to all on Twitter a few years back. That's the way it should be: Put it out there for all shops to respond to, but don't make it an exercise that consumes agency resources for three weeks.

 There's a famous blogger in Paris called Joe La Pompe (a generic nickname that's kind of like "Joe the Copycat") who, for 15 years, has been calling out ad copycats that send their work to big award shows. This guy has ruined careers, and many people feel he's cultivated a kind of hysterical witch-hunting of even vaguely similar creative ideas (which are inevitable).

But if you actually talk to him, it's surprising to find out how much of a relativist he is. He still believes creativity is defined by an effort to be different and inventive, and if advertising wants to hold itself to the standard of creativity, it has to assume that responsibility. But he also knows that people are pressed for time, that the young people who most often populate agencies lack experience and knowledge about how much has been done before, and—most critically—sometimes the same idea just happens, and it's because advertising itself may cultivate the tendency.

The way he sees it, advertising is all about riding an existing cultural trend, like selfies. So if your whole business is about copying what's already in the air, you're going to end up with a lot of similar work (there are probably 20 pet food campaigns that feature dog selfies. Seriously).

"The robb'd that smiles, steals something from the thief; He robs himself that spends a bootless grief."

WILLIAM SHAKESPEARE

47.

Can a successful creative culture be imported to a satellite agency?

Allowing for regional influences.

It can but it has to be done carefully. Netflix has done it in multiple countries with a certain amount of success. I think they've managed to do it because they've written out what's important to the company and drummed it into everyone who comes through the door. Country offices all interact closely with corporate and are trained at headquarters. It wouldn't surprise me if part of their performance relied on ensuring they convey the culture effectively when managing local agencies—because agencies get a lot of training on what Netflix values both creatively and in terms of interaction with partners.

This isn't as creepy as it sounds; honestly, they watch for and limit behaviors I wish most people cared about. One rule of agency collaboration was basically "if you ever smell politics behind a decision, tell us immediately." They want that shit nipped in the bud the second it rears its head, and if an agency can't play nice in good faith and is a repeat offender, it's off the books without a second glance.

It's a good model to follow. I think agencies can fall into the trap of thinking their culture is magic and can sustain itself on its own, but I'd follow Netflix: Values require training from leadership, ownership of those values, clear accountability, and a close relationship with the Mothership and partners.

So tough. I don't know that I've ever succeeded in a grand way with this, though I've tried. Having some thread of culture is important. Something that everyone can look up to and hold as the bar we aspire to reach. But then you've got to allow for individual, regional and cultural influences. Unique personalities are brought to each team, so cramming some doctrine down their throats never works. Great leadership knows when to guide, when to inspire, and when to step back and let people do their thing.

Brands are different animals. Way easier to spin a few branches off a retailer or insurance company because the Mothership dictates every aspect of office life. Ad agencies that open up in different locations, of course, have to follow the lead of the parent company, but deviate in terms of local clients and how that local culture informs who they are.

I think you can socialize and share company-wide learnings from sister agencies, but each shop also needs to feel it has the autonomy to do things its way, lest it feel like the latest Best Buy that just opened in a new city.

48.

Where do you find the will to do stuff that doesn't interest you?

Pretending.

I tell a story in my head. When I was little and my parents made me clean the yard, I pretended to be a little boy on a farm doing a PBS special about my life, with cameras following me while I raked and explained the importance of all my chores. I cleaned long into dusk.

 There is nothing that I could possibly say that would top Angela's response to this question. So from now on, I will picture myself as a little boy on a farm, doing a PBS special about my life...

 The boring stuff is offset by the lottery ticket hope that the next project to grace our desks will be the career-defining one. To think otherwise is to give up.

"I can't account for how at any given moment I feel the need to explore life as opposed to another, but I do know that I can only do this work if I feel almost as if there is no choice; that a subject coincides inexplicably with a very personal need and a very specific moment in time."

DANIEL DAY-LEWIS

49.

Do you procrastinate?

I was too
busy to
answer this
question.

I once read a study that found we're addicted to procrastination because we actually do work better under pressure.

That doesn't stop me from trying to be a better planner (with about an 80% fail rate). I fall into the "ritual" trap a lot—like, if I can just do this then this and this, I'll be ready to work. Sometimes that works: Like when I find just the right spot on the couch and have tea beside me. Sometimes I blow a whole day getting all anal about things I never normally care about—like whoa, deadline? But it's such a good day to clean the couch!

When I'm getting too ritually, probably the best thing to do is break out of it, open the goddamn computer and plunge myself into the work. It'll sort itself out once I'm inside the task, you know? It's like ordering a salad: You never want to, but you're perfectly fine with it once it arrives.

 I was too busy to answer this question.

 When I'm done procrastinating I'll answer this. For now, see my answer re: Creative process. I actually do need to do certain things in a certain order for me to feel comfortable enough to start the actual process.

"Procrastination is the art of keeping up with yesterday."

DON MARQUIS

50.
How long to procrastinate?

Until...

Until you really feel the barrel of the gun against your temple.

 Yep.

 When the clock looks at you and says, "Hey man, I've done all I can. We're presenting in four hours. It's all on you now."

"MY CREATIVE PROCESS IS QUITE SLOW. I HEAR MELODIES IN MY HEAD WHILE I'M WASHING THE DISHES AND I ALLOW MY SUBCONSCIOUS TO DO THE WORK."

SINÉAD O'CONNOR

51.

How do you manage creative adversity?

My most creative times have come from personal turmoil.

When you're dealing with trouble in personal life and your career is based on being a creative, how do you tune it out? Do you find solace in the work? Are you distracted? Each creative has a ritual or headspace they seem to need to get into before starting their brainstorm, or creative work, and they can easily be distracted by things that aren't going well. My most creative times have come from personal turmoil. I suspect it's that way for many people in this business.

 I've had moments when some existential problem becomes a creative opportunity. I'm mulling over it after days of sleeplessness, my emotions rising to the surface and making my head all hot … and suddenly a narrative spins through. I have to rush to a computer or grab a pen and get it all down. It writes itself, like a ballet I have to follow and pin to a permanent place. When I've finally finished, I feel exorcised.

The most counterproductive problems, though, are banal: A relationship fight, a bad day at work. I set it aside and focus on little things I can get done that won't require too much braining. If I feel too useless, I take a long lunch and try sorting that shit out so I can come back effective—whether that means writing down talking points, or just calling the goddamn person and finishing whatever match we're trying to win.

I've had my share of personal issues while running agencies—family deaths, divorce, cancer. The truth is, everyone has adversity. What really matters is how they handle it. For some people, a relationship breakup can weigh as heavy as a cancer diagnosis for another person. Everyone processes personal stress and situations differently, and there's no acceptable scale that says how we're each supposed to act when we're doled out something difficult to deal with.

I believe that culture and recruitment are key here. The best teams are chock full of people that can bring a smile to the office regardless of what is going on in their personal life. These are the people that are more fun to work with, have a healthier mental state and are ultimately more productive. A sad sack in the office brings the whole team down, and nobody wants to deal with that. When you hire, hire people who can get through the worst and still deliver their best.

If you're hit with something really bad, go home. And stay home for as long as you need to. You're doing your entire team a disservice while you power through martyrdom with a miserable attitude, claiming "I'll be okay, I'll be okay." These people believe they're viewed as troopers, and instead they kill the vibe for everyone. Take the time you need, and then when you're ready, show up with a positive attitude, ready for action. The entire team will be there for you.

 You know that saying "It's not personal; it's business"? Really, so much of business is personal. It's even deeply personal. If I can get by on a shit day, a lot of it is because I know I can trust people or the process. The truth is, when things start to get hard at work, I really need other people to help share the load.

People shouldn't have to feel like they're facing a shit situation in a vacuum. There's so much sucky stuff in life we have to face alone, and work shouldn't be one of those things you feel like you have to "survive."

"LIFE IS LOSS.
FREQUENT, USUAL LOSS."

JILL ALEXANDER ESSBAUM

52.

How do you cultivate creativity in a negative environment?

Get out.

Or change.

267

Get out.

Or change.

In *An Astronaut's Guide to Life on Earth*, Chris Hadfield talks about how goddamn hard it is to be an astronaut. You study forever to be the best and put your life at constant risk. When you're finally among the upper echelons of astronauts, you have to keep learning, keep optimizing, keep advancing, and you might never even fly. Some astronauts might go into space four times, and most who go up only do once. The majority just never do. But they have to keep at it, keep smiling, keep supporting their teams, because who knows. So it's rough.

Then there's the matter of finally being in space and facing an emergency. Hadfield stresses the importance of maintaining a positive attitude all the time, no matter what, because one negative vibe can domino through the entire team and literally get everybody killed.

I guess the point is, lift up the places you're in. Having worked in negative environments, I recognize the consequences: I didn't do my best work, lived in fear, poisoned my homelife. Negativity poisons everything. It's okay to cut out when the culture is bad; you can feel it when a place is rejecting you or you're rejecting it. You don't win anything by staying. You just kind of break down. (Like in space!)

(My therapist finds it worrying that I navigate my life by

imagining I'm in near-death conditions out of orbit.)

 Get out, or change the environment. For me, nothing is more important than a positive attitude. If you can't control or dramatically affect the negative environment that you're in, do everything in your power to remove yourself from it. Nothing good will come from these places, and if it does, it's the exception. Usually followed by more negativity. Positivity breeds ideas, fun, productivity and success.

 It starts with knowing if you can win that battle in the first place. It's one thing to come in and try and turn around a creative department. It's another if your efforts are doomed before you start because the agency owner is the problem, and anything you do will be rendered moot. If you have no choice and are stuck in an environment that needs creative CPR, seek out footholds where you can, and build from there. Nurture chemistry between people where you find even the tiniest bit, and above all else, don't get caught up in the negativity of others. Seek out those will be your best advocates and keep them close.

"I'VE NEVER RESPONDED WELL TO ENTRENCHED NEGATIVE THINKING."
DAVID BOWIE

53.

How do you deal with failure?

Letting go.

There are a couple of things I've done that, when I think back on them, give me that white-cold feeling. I have only once been fired for doing something genuinely stupid (Starbucks, age sixteen: Asking a general whether he'd ever killed anyone. He called the store, then the district, then the region, then Seattle. Seattle dropped me and I can never work there again.)

I am terrified of failure, which is funny because as the American in Paris I'm always talking about the importance of embracing it, being open to and okay with it. France has a more formal and in some cases less forgiving culture than US startup culture. But the truth is, I am SUPER not okay with my failures. They turn me into a neurotic puddle of misery-mud.

I am trying to get over this—assessing failure, rolling out what we can do better next time, and what we learned. You can't live your life tiptoeing over eggshells, so I cut failures up into little pieces that I don't have to be scared of: What happened. What I learned. How to do better next time. Steps to fix it if it's fixable. Remember that being scared shitless means you'll 99% never ever EVER do it again, and that's priceless.

 Let it go. It passes. It hurts so bad, it's embarrassing, it cost you money, a relationship, a job or more. But if you're still alive, you can pick yourself up and move forward. I always try to quickly analyze what went wrong, what I could have done differently, and what can I learn from a particular failure. Then I let it go. Dwelling on failures creates a victim mentality, a lack of confidence and negative energy that doesn't accomplish anything. Always remember that there are greater people who have made grander failures. Everything's going to be okay.

 I hate losing. I'll learn from it and move on, but I hate it. When our team walks into a pitch, I don't care what other agency we're up against, I believe we can't lose. It's disappointing if we do, but I never walk in thinking we will lose. When a client walks, I ask what we could have done better and why didn't we do it.

54.

How do you know when you've gotten too comfortable?

Scare

yourself.

At some point I knew I was too comfortable when I started shooting down the ideas of the bright-eyed newbies that invaded my company. It was like, "Oh my god, I'm killing them and I don't even know why. I need to get out of here."

 Do something that scares you on a regular basis. The longer you are comfortable, the more creativity you kill.

 Fear is a really good rule of thumb. I think when you start fearing what's outside your agency walls, or fearing what might happen if you took this leap, you're probably too comfortable. One girl I worked with quit to start her own café. She told me she drummed up the courage to quit when she realized she was scared of what would happen if she left. It got her thinking, "A year ago, I applied for this agency job, and I didn't even really know what I was applying for. I wasn't scared at all. What happened to me?!"

 I want to feel comfortable relative to how good we are as a team. There's tremendous comfort in knowing that you're part of a team of uniquely talented people who can bring it creatively, because it keeps you on your toes. But it also builds trust. I've been places where management shuffles up teams just when people have gelled and I've never seen it work well after, or at least it wasn't the same. You see this type of consistency in other fields like film or music, where people often use the same production crews or assistants. Clint Eastwood uses the same group of production people for most of his films. Bands work with the same engineers, producers and agents for the same reason. This goes back to chemistry. Give me chemistry first.

Where comfort turns to complacency is in your creative output. If you keep milking the same style and forget about innovation somewhere in the food chain, you're selling yourself short because people want to be excited by what you do.

 I feel you on random shuffles. I once worked for a guy like that—he'd move people around or randomly change titles, or even the structure of the agency, just for the sake of change. We had a 100% turnover rate; nobody felt safe, nobody felt like they could invest in the role they'd been given because who knew if it would be there in six months? You do need to feel safe, and comfortable with who you're working with, to perform well.

55.

**Have you got
a Plan B?**

No cushion.

I don't have a plan B at the moment, but I'm always working on one. Actually, I like to approach every single decision that I make with an understanding of all available options, and a worst case scenario. I've always believed that if you can mentally—or physically— prepare yourself for the worst case scenario, you'll always be okay. So I guess my plan B is accepting the worst case scenario.

Did we always know we wanted to create? Or was mom right and that we needed a backup plan? Working at a home improvement store may offer great benefits, but nurturing your creative spirit ain't one of them. The art director who stays at a shitty agency for 10 years because they hope things will get better. Or perhaps it's the notion that they can find something else—nay, better, which keeps them from leaving. Shame on the agency that fosters either scenario.

What about the person who leaves this business to pursue a completely different field altogether? Eric Proulx explored this dynamic perfectly in *Lemonade.*

Whether you get thrown into sudden career option mode via the long walk to your immediate supervisor's office, or you've planned to turn that side jewelry business into your thing, the notion of a plan B is always there for many. Or is it?

 France valorizes salaried workers, so for a long time I thought I needed a salary to prove I'm well-integrated, that I can commit, that somebody wants me. But a couple of years ago, plugging along with my regular clients, whom I like a lot, I realized I love freelance and don't want to give it up. It lets me evolve and focus on other types of work when I need to take a break from something else. It exposes me to new opportunities more often than one job would. My skills have evolved alongside my clients' changing demands.

For the last several years I've had about five regular gigs, one of which is basically full-time and really demanding. It is hard, but also great: They're all projects and people I love working with. And I like knowing that it isn't one thing that defines my professional life; it's many. Also, I think I'd have to seriously fuck up to lose all of them at once. I have spread my risk.

So I guess I'm the type of person who does Plan A, B, C, D and E simultaneously. Also, I save a fixed percent of money from all my takings—so if I lose something or want to leave a place, I have a cushion to consider options if needed.

56.

When do you walk away?

When indeed.

I have a very bad "walking away" track record. I really hate confrontation and really like responsibility.

This is how I've come to define when it's time for me to walk away: When I dread waking up in the morning, when the work starts piling up and I've lost the motivation to keep up. Once the presence of those symptoms is noted, and avenues of resolution exhausted, there's nothing for it but to scoop up my balls and call it a day.

I often get hung up on what I'll say to justify departure. Sometimes there's no "great big opportunity" that scoops you up and makes it easy to justify ("I have to go; I just got the job of my dreams!"). Sometimes you just have to go because there's nothing left to contribute. That's the scariest.

I am still not sure what to say in cases like this that won't make me sound like a flippant teenager breaking up with her boyfriend in front of the lockers ("It's just me"—hand up, hair toss, heels clicking to punctuate departure). But I can't emphasize enough the importance of knowing when to stop. When I left my last agency, I told the CD the truth—that I love this place but I think we've run our course—and he understood and supported me. I felt lucky to be able to do that.

We've been drilled into believing that the stupidest thing you can do in this career-driven age is leave without having another job lined up. It's like being a serial monogamist. How do you know who you are, and what you really want, until you've spent some time alone, forced to come up with your own unassigned objectives?

I think we all dislike confrontation and want structure-slash-responsibility. Why are we creatives so passive-aggressive at times? Is it linked to how we are more sensitive and pick up on subtleties that others miss? I either embrace or blame it on my ENFJ-ness.

When to walk? When we decide enough's enough.

As Patrick Swayze's Dalton notes in *Road House*, "Nothin' I ain't used to, but then it's amazing what you can get used to."

Let's take that further and say it's amazing what you can talk yourself into. When warning signs are all over the place, channel your inner *Blink* and think back to the first time you met the account person who would ultimately make your life a living hell. There was something about them that you overlooked as you basked in the glow of the agency tour, including the kitchen and tequila cart.

But in hindsight, your gut was right, wasn't it? Yet you took the job.

So why do we stay in relationships that we know we need to get out of? I get that perhaps it's a bit loaded, maybe it's even an unfair question, because some people don't necessarily have the means to move on at that point in time. Lack of money, resources or support are legit reasons for staying put. But don't we tell women to get out of abusive relationships? That there's always somewhere to go? Of course we do.

Now, there are more subtle things at work in a bad work environment in terms of what we consider abuse. We get lulled into thinking things aren't that bad because, well, nobody's yelling at me and they do give me a check every few weeks or so, right? But this is the problem: Death by a thousand billable hours, all in an effort to make someone else well-off. And we never see it until it's too late. Watch Erik Proulx's Lemonade for a look at pursuing one's dreams before it's too late for you.

 I'm with Angela on this: if you can't wake up in the morning excited about your day, then it's time to give your career some serious re-evaluation. I'm guilty of staying in situations longer than I should have, and like Angela (and most creatives, I believe), avoid confrontation. Age has given me a sort of wisdom here, and I'm careful now to always communicate honestly about the relationships that I'm in, and call out any issues or missed expectations. The older I get, the less patient I am. In a great way. I'm quick to get out of a bad situation today, and that wasn't the case when I was younger. Experience also gives you the vision to see a bad situation, rather than make excuses for it. I've learned that the more honest you are with the people around you, the less you'll find yourself in confrontational situations. Always move toward happiness.

 I have a longtime fantasy about being either **fuck-you rich** or **fuck-you old**. I think what I'm trying to get to is **fuck you**, full stop.

Early on in my career I had a bad day at work and ended up in the kitchen, passive aggressively eating all the butter cookies. The graphic designer—a more experienced woman—walked in, took a look at me and said, "When you're older, you'll hit a point when you're sure of what you can do, sure of what you want to do, and sure of what you want to say no to."

It was so frustrating to know that she was right, and that knowing it wasn't enough to get me there. Some things only come with time, and time can be a slow-ass tunnel.

In retrospect though, I might have assumed too readily that she was intuiting my work issues. Maybe she was just talking about the cookies.

MOST ALL OF US

"DON'T EVER ASK ME AGAIN WHY I'M
NOT IN VAN HALEN. I WAS THROWN OUT,
I WAS STABBED IN THE BACK AND LEFT
FOR DEAD. AND YOU JUST CAN'T GO BACK
AND HUG AND KISS THOSE KIND
OF PEOPLE THAT DO THAT TO YOU."

SAMMY HAGAR

"THEY WERE BECOMING IMPATIENT WITH HIM AT LAST. TOLERANCE IS A QUESTION OF PATIENCE, AND PATIENCE
IS A QUESTION OF NERVES, AND THEIR NERVES WERE STRAINED."

GRAHAM GREENE

57.

When do you pursue new things?

We have

so much

opportunity

at our

fingertips.

At first glance this might seem like a twist on the question about walking away, but not really. If you look at the music industry you'll see an interesting phenomenon occur with musicians who embrace this idea. Look at the case of Bon Iver and founder Justin Vernon. He started Volcano Choir after feeling he had said all he could say with the incarnation of Bon Iver:

"I don't really write songs anymore. The last Bon Iver record was a very 'sitting down with a guitar and writing' kind of record ... I really have to be in a specific headspace to even begin to illuminate an idea that would create another Bon Iver record, and I'm just not there ... I'm really honoured that Bon Iver gives me a platform to do whatever I want, but there's only so much time you can spend digging through yourself before you become insular. I'm not in a hurry to go back to that temperature. All of the music I've been making shifting away from Bon Iver feels really good ... so if I ever do go back to Bon Iver it will be all the better for it."

This introduces several dynamics into the mix. First, when your audience wants you to continue in the same vein, what do you do? In the same way that repeating a formula that made you money makes them comfortable, it kills the artist who wants to pursue different directions and grow. In the advertising and marketing world, we're paid to tell clients what they need to hear, but ultimately, we're also paid to give them what they want.

This is made worse for the artist where compensation is involved because you often have A) Demanding fans wanting more of the same, B) A record company wanting more of the same and C) You the artist not caring about money as a primary motivator. Some do, of course, but there is a point you reach where compromise, commerce and creativity all meet. Artists in galleries deal with this all the time as well: The gallerist can "sell" more of your red paintings but you aren't feeling it.

What's the point at which you compromise or say fuck it?

 I took a pop culture course in college and we spent about a week studying fandom: How it killed Elvis, hardened Sinatra, stopped the Beatles from continuing to perform live, and would eventually kill Michael Jackson.

The teacher said fandom is dangerous because it's basically mob hysteria, and the money it attracts forces handlers to transform you, the product, into a non-evolving caricature of yourself. Every time Elvis tried to evolve, somebody would go, "do that cute thing you do. Just that thing, that's what people want."

You can see how this affected him when you watch his last Unplugged show, to which only an intimate group of old friends and fans were invited. He strums his guitar, plays a few old hits, and gently makes fun of himself. He is lovely, kind and sad. He is living a tragedy he can't define. Next thing we know, he's dead.

I am torn between the importance of mastering something so completely that I belong to it and it to me, and letting myself pursue all the things this brave new world avails. We have so much opportunity at our fingertips, so many ways to be reborn.

An older friend told me that young people have no conception about how long life truly is, and we behave as if every decision we make will be fixed for always. I know I have a tendency to clench my fist and let the sand run through. And while I may never get to the point where I just throw open my hands and run, I think I can loosen my grip. It's about letting myself live in that delicate space between making mindful decisions but also embracing and accepting what comes.

Even if you can't be the best concert pianist the world has ever seen, you can still learn the piano, and it will add a richesse to your life that you didn't have before. Eric Proulx's Lemonade taught us that a full career in advertising doesn't have to stop you from going off and doing something completely different later on, no matter how old you are or what people say. As in enterprises, so in life: The adventure doesn't stop just because you pivot. It often becomes a better one.

To wit, this whole collaboration started as a "new thing"—a podcast Bill wanted to try out, years ago. We recorded a powerful conversation on racism in advertising with Hadji Williams and suddenly realized we'd created something that was important to us, and potentially to other people.

Out of nothing. Out of just reaching out and recording a chat. And it's been seven years, then Darryl came on board because we've always wanted to do something together, and here we are now, trying something else new. It's crazy.

 I feel like I've had at least three careers in my life. None were really planned in advance, and most were opportunities that presented themselves at one time or another. I think it's important to keep an open mind to who you are, who you might be in the future, and always explore new interests. You should always pursue new things. What's perceived as a waste of time at the moment (or by outsiders) nearly always comes with a lesson or two, so even if the thing you've pursued fails, you've grown as a person.

It wasn't until much later in life that I got the opportunity to live outside of the US. I wish that I had more aggressively pursued this when I was younger. What I learned in a single year, at the end of my career, has been more life-changing than nearly anything I did in my career prior. You never know what's going to change your life forever, but you can bet that it starts by pursuing something new.

"You have brains in your head. You have feet in your shoes. You can steer yourself in any direction you choose."

DR. SEUSS

58.

**Would you do
it all again?**

Hindsight

is

everything.

Of course. But I'd change some things. Age and experience begets a wisdom of sorts.

Hindsight is everything. If I could do it all again, I'd make more moves. I'm not convinced that long-term loyalty paid off for me. I held two of my positions for at least ten years each.

That's a significant part of my life devoted to individual companies. Had I taken different positions every two or three years instead, I would have added several additional positions to my CV. That experience might have taught me more about people, workplaces, and process at a faster pace. I eventually learned all of this, but who knows how my career might have been impacted if I could have compressed that experience into three years?

Everything else? Absolutely, definitely. All my life I got to be the dude who loved his job. How many people do you know who love their jobs? No matter how hard or long I've worked, I can't say I've really ever "worked" a hard day. Even at the most miserable agency where I was employed, at the end of the day, what was I doing? Directing a photoshoot? Brainstorming? Even writing PowerPoint decks won't break you into a sweat. Try telling a highway worker or roofer how stressful your day was, or how horrible it is that you're working 12 hour days, and see what sympathy you get. Sometimes I can't fathom that we get paid money to do what we do for a living.

So yes, I'd sign up for this mission over and over and over again.

 I play this game in my head a lot now. I take what I should have, didn't or couldn't know before but do now, and try and apply it to my life through my children. Not just with the business aspect of things (although with a daughter who's an art director, she gets more than a few shortcuts sent her way), but from a life POV. Seeing relationships for what they are and learning to recognize the good ones—and bad ones—is a far more valuable service I can provide them.

This gives the topic a bear-hug like nothing else, because if creativity is informed by anything, it's relationships. To our colleagues, to the client, to the work; to the cold, hard, dead, unforgiving surface, substrate or ether that we aspire to make something happen in or on. To the critic of the work, the work to the artist ... all of it. This cause and effect never diminishes, even if you hole up in a cave with a volleyball on a deserted isle and nobody ever sees another thing you do, ever ... Wilson always taunts. Always.

In college I had a job at a startup, where they plucked me out of customer support and saddled me with the development of a marketing department. Around that time, I changed my major from English to Mass Comm. About a year into the gig, I started writing for Adrants.

I was young when I got into the business. I didn't know much when I started writing about advertising, and felt like I was at a huge disadvantage: I was critiquing work, and an industry at large, that I knew nothing about outside of books, media, conferences and my own feelings about advertising. I was sure that at some point, somebody would call me out on it.

To illustrate how terribly little I knew, at one point a creative who won an award told me that her project was a Rube Goldberg. I was like, "What's that?" and she just stared at me like I was an alien and repeated, "It's a Rube Goldberg." I knew what one was, but I'd never heard its name.

Moments like that made me want to absorb as much as I could. I started working with agencies, consultants and brands to learn both my role and those of others. I spent more time on Wikipedia and second-guessed my knowledge of things before knocking them. I followed projects closely; I wanted to know everything I didn't know.

I've come a reasonably long way, but every day the knowledge base changes, which is the nature of advertising, journalism and technology. All told, this industry, which has historically been hard on women, minorities and the aging, has been kind to me. I like to think it's because I am open, earnest and good at what I do, and people recognize that.

When I changed countries, I was working for both MarketingVox and Adrants. Three months into my move, they both laid me off after the market collapsed. But people recognized my work from the States and drew me under their wings. I could have drowned on the other side of the world without a network or a real shot, and I didn't, because advertising took care of its own. Most of the people I work with have become good friends, and if it weren't for this industry and everything I've done, I would never have met Bill and Darryl, who are two of my best.

If you happen to be in advertising, or to be interested in the profession, be proud of that choice: Advertising is stressful, but it's also one of the funnest, most dynamic and rewarding jobs you can have. I can think of few other professions where every weird thing you're into can be used, where you have to play sociologist, strategist and data analyst, where you can get paid for transforming shower-time reflection into a living, breathing concept.

It gets a lot of knocks for superficiality. But it also bears a huge cultural responsibility that it didn't ask for and doesn't always assume: It teaches us how to be kids, tweens, teens, adults. It tells us what social badges to use to convey the messages we want in life. It's a reflection of what a culture values and fears.

So don't ever let anyone give you shit about working in this industry. It attracts a lot of megalomaniacs, but it needs people who care about it—people who care about what massive, community-impacting corporations are trying to say.

But it's also important to be a relativist: We're not curing cancer. When the water gets hot, take a step back and breathe. Don't let your friends and family be slain on the altar of a goddamn cereal jingle. And try to be a force for good. The right people will always find you, and you them.

So yes. I'd do it again and again.

"IT TAKES A LONG TIME FOR MEN TO ACQUIRE THEIR PARTICULAR COUNTENANCES. IT IS AS IF THEY WERE BORN WITHOUT THEIR FACES, THEIR FOREHEADS, THEIR NOSES OR THEIR EYES. THEY ACQUIRE ALL THESE WITH THE PASSAGE OF TIME, AND ONE MUST BE PATIENT; IT TAKES TIME BEFORE EVERYTHING IS PROPERLY ASSEMBLED."

JOSEPH ROTH

creative

horizons

"Last words before bowing out."

ALL OF US

Creativity is an elusive beast.

Try and pin it down and you'll get bit. That's because it means something different to everyone you ask. The gallery owner, musician, art director, account person, marketing director and customer each have an opinion. Take us: Three souls riffing on 58 aspects of the topic relative to our industry alone, and look how varied our responses are.

Sum up its essence in a sentence, I double dare you. I can't because I don't subscribe to the notion that the "answer" for anything can be found in a single absolute. One exception, however, was my art school classmate, who, when answering the semester's final exam question "What is Zen?" Simply wrote "Zen is..." on his paper, turned it in a few minutes later, then promptly walked out.

For that inspired piece of creativity, he got an A+.

This sounds like something Gertrude Stein did in college: She wrote something like "I don't feel a bit like an examination paper in philosophy today" over the top of an exam and left. A+. Great minds?

Before you eye roll unmercifully, it's precisely that dynamic which allows the notion of creativity to meld with however we experience it, make it our own, and in turn define it.

When we began this project, we thought about topics we'd love to discuss that would give someone reason enough to spend time with us in book form. It was only after Darryl proposed a direction focused on defining what creativity is that the AdVerve experience became unified for us in several ways.

First, creativity has been the one thread in the proverbial quilt of all the shows we've covered to this point, from ageism to music piracy to Twilight's infiltration of the global teen zeitgeist. Secondly, it opened the discussion beyond our little world to now include you, the dear reader, because it's not just our topic.

Creativity is everyone's.

When we started this, we were a bit nervous. Our walks of life have been very different, but in the end we're all working in advertising. The question was how to convey messages that could be useful to people from all walks of life.

Bill is right: Creativity is everyone's, and its interpretation will differ based on all kinds of factors. What we all want to say is that there isn't a right or wrong way to do this. Trust yourself. Chase your interests. Hone your instincts. Listen to your gut; it's your subconscious's way of telling you what it needs to thrive. Give yourself outlets.

In a way, advertising might be one of the ideal ways of approaching creativity, because it's ephemeral. I can't think of anything truer to life than that: There's something noble about working in a space where the best of you will be demanded on a regular basis, without the pretentious notion it will last forever. Nothing does. That doesn't mean it shouldn't kick ass, shouldn't enrich a human moment.

I have been diagnosed with an incurable cancer, which I fight as I write these very words. This position has given me great insight to life, the work that I've done, the relationships that I've grown (or ended), the companies that I've launched, assisted, projects completed, accolades achieved, the people that I've led and the leaders who have led me. I've given great thought to my life to date, and here's what I've learned: So much of it doesn't matter.

What doesn't matter: Client wins, the awards, job titles, the money, the way other people rank you or your work. What matters: The life experience. The love, smiles, laughs, things learned, the creativity that makes remarkable moments. Creativity solves problems, teaches new perspectives, gives us hope and dreams, and makes things happen that might otherwise seem impossible. When you're fighting for your life, you could care less about the added features to a new laundry detergent. But you'll cherish work that makes you proud, fun moments that led to brilliance, and relationships that grew past a conference room.

Search for creativity. Support creativity. Fight for creativity. Creativity is the one thing you may look back on as the thread that sews together the most important aspects of your entire life.

And then you'll die.

WITHOUT THESE FOLKS, THIS WOULDN'T HAVE HAPPENED...

TO OUR ADVERVE OLDIES: Joe Jaffe, Mike McSunas, Howie Goldfarb, Jeff Kwiatek, Dave 'Where's My Jetpack?' Wilkie, Chris Havranek, George Parker, Åsk Wäppling, Hal Thomas, Joe La Pompe, Saul Colt, FrédG Léveque, Ben Kunz, Helen Klein Ross, Bob Knorpp, Hadji Williams, Copyranter, Sandmonkey, Deb Wiseman and to all our many podcast guests. We wouldn't have anything to build on without you. And if we missed naming any of you, sorry. We're getting old. Or you never sent us an email (we like email!), in which case this is strictly your fault.

TO OUR LOVERS: Kat, Melissa, and Romain for listening to us talk smack for hours once a week for over a year.

TO THE HATERS: Thanks for hate-reading! We hope you paid full price.

NEED MORE OF US? FIND YOU SOME:

mtlb

luckthelady

darrylohrt

adverve

advervepodcast@gmail.com

Made in the USA
San Bernardino, CA
26 January 2020